Thoughts

To Dolores,

Positive 'thoughts' always
and Best Wishes.

Ben

Ben Carnevale

PAGE PUBLISHING
Conneaut Lake, PA

First originally published by Page Publishing 2024

ISBN 979-8-89315-046-9 (hc)
ISBN 979-8-89315-045-2 (digital)

Printed in the United States of America

To my wonderful wife, Joanne, for her support and unconditional love.

Contents

Preface

I was born and grew up in Newton, Massachusetts, in 1933, and like many other children, I was faced with my share of disappointments and discouragements…it's part of growing up. Part of life, right? Although I'm a very active individual and have been throughout my life, retirement gave me the opportunity to pause and reflect into my past, as well as the opportunity to evaluate and learn. My discouragements and disappointments resulted in who and what I am today. I wrote this book to address these specific issues, and my hope is that the reader will also pause and realize that the simple "thoughts" we encounter are not to be dismissed, but rather a path along our lives, which results in who and what we are. Positive thoughts might just be the answer.

I think we're missing out on something very important. We go about our days expecting or at least hoping that every day goes as planned. I have heard and have seen people become disturbed, discouraged, and even upset, ending up saying things they may later regret. After being there, done that myself, I have learned a few things as to how such situations come about. They seem spontaneous, as though this behavior is the "norm." Why wouldn't it be?

Who is Joanne Blum-Carnevale? Born in Dansville, New York, Joanne is the most wonderful, talented, attractive, generous, and caring person I have ever known! She recently entered Marquis Who's Who in America publication. She was the daughter of medical professionals, and during her career as a certified registered nurse anesthetist (CRNA), she devoted forty years giving anesthesia in hospital operating rooms…a medical professional, now retired.

But why am I telling you this? Joanne was highly respected by the OR surgeons and surgical staffs, especially due to her unique relationships with her very young patients. Her approach in administrating anesthesia to her patients was my principal motivation for writing this book. She created positive thoughts within her young patients, which always resulted in successful surgery outcomes.

I became deeply emotional during testimonies given by OR surgeons at her retirement celebration. Rephrasing one surgeon's testimonial: "Joanne was exceptional and will be deeply missed by the entire OR staff. She would always lead the OR staff into a song with her young patients, followed by a dialogue while preparing them for anesthesia. Joanne would explain to them in her special and comforting voice, assuring them that 'if you think of something that you really, really like, you will wake up with a big smile on your face!'" I will never forget that memorable evening. Joanne has been my special friend and dear wife since 1987.

Acknowledgments

Thank you to Joanne Blum-Carnevale for the countless hours of enjoyable and interesting discussions we had about our beautiful planet, our fascinating careers, our amazing environment, and above all, our incredible wildlife.

To Page Publishing for promptness, professionalism, and perfection.

To warm- and cold-blooded animals and insects for sharing your unique lives with me and with the entire world. Each of you have a special purpose in our lives. Thank you for your vital contribution to our environment; we could not exist without you. You have given us the inspiration to not only learn more about you but to also have "thoughts" about the ongoing difficulties and challenges you experience moment by moment in raising your families, protecting against dangers, challenges of survival, searching for food, and providing shelter.

To the environment for providing me, and the entire world, with the necessary ingredients to not only exist but also for your marvelous wonders and for your spectacular sights all around and within your beautiful and amazing planet. I am saturated with countless positive "thoughts" about all that you have given. Indeed "the best things in life are free."

To my Creator, thank you for everything, and I mean everything…you have given me the very, very best and most beautiful of all wonders and sights that I could ever experience, and that I could ever imagine. You have given me the best and dearest friends and relatives, the most wonderful people I have met, and the best and most beautiful places I have ever been. However undeservingly, they were abundantly, unconditionally, and freely given to me. You have given me the knowledge, wisdom, and patience to face the many challenges in writing this…my third book. Thank you all!

Introduction

This is a novel about thoughts that influences our decisions, which determines the types of lives we live. Decisions from those we come in contact with, those we never met, never known, or never even knew existed also affects our thought process. To some extent, we all realize and understand that the decisions which we make affects our quality of life, our destiny, and how the decisions of others affect our lives in a similar manner. We get it! But do we really understand how and how *often* this happens and the *frequency* of occurrences? So do we really get it?

Although it appears to be oblivious to some extent, I believe our actions may prove otherwise. We may be sitting outside at a train station or on a park bench staring at our smartphone and without realizing it a cigar smoker decides to sit next to us. Preoccupied with our smartphone, the wind direction may be acceptable to some but to others tells us that it's time to move. After evaluating our reason to move, we stumble over several thoughts, which may or may not take priority over our existing thoughts. Our planned or unplanned day has now changed.

Jainism religion (Jain monks), as well as other religions, avoids stepping on ants in their belief to protect all living matter. In addition to respecting their religious belief, it's my belief that during such "lifesaving events," thought events are also being produced, voluntarily or involuntarily, another avenue shaping our lives.

When your child disobeys, why not get angry? When your spouse messes things up, why not take the opportunity for anger? Many of us regretfully behave in such a manner even if not to this extent. Hopefully, we'll understand there's a reason these events happen to a point where they may even become beneficial!

It wasn't until after my retirement that I was able to focus on the things that really mattered. I mean "that really mattered." I seriously began thinking about how I got here and how I got this far. I began to realize that simple interruptions in my typical everyday thoughts caused my thought process to shift gears. Interruptions resulting from dialogues with other people, phone calls, or simply looking at something at random, such as an animal, a sports figure, and a host of other examples.

These indeed can change our chain of thought, causing us to ask ourselves…are we now heading in a different path because of a change in our thoughts? I found my thought concepts amazing! To me, this was the answer to the why and how we got here.

Chapter 1

My Thoughts Concept

Introduction

The decisions that we make not only affect our lives but may directly or indirectly affect the lives of many others. And the decisions made by others may affect our lives as well. But what are decisions? How are they created? And how do we acquire them? I believe my thoughts concept has a lot to do with the answers to these questions. Examples throughout this book may allow the reader to understand just how much our larger *macro thoughts* can play a pivotal role in determining the quality of our lives as well our destinies. And the very small thoughts, which I call *micro thoughts*, can also result in major changes in our lives as well as in the lives of others. Too often we think about, and we decide upon everyday events without realizing the benefits or consequences of the outcome.

I sincerely believe that every thought we have during our lifetime, whether macro or micro, determines our quality of life and our destinies. For this is what our lives are all about, from our alpha to our omega…a series of thoughts that shape the type of person that we are at any present time, the type of person we will become, our character, personalities, successes, friendships, education, family, and our destiny.

Our Brain

How does our brain allow us to think? Among the many elements responsible for the functions of our brain are neurons. They are the basic cells in our brain which transmit information to other nerve cells in the form of electrical impulses. Our brain primarily consists of an estimated one hundred billion neuron cells. These cells release chemicals that trigger electrical impulses, which allow communications within our brain that are responsible for our thought process.

Studies explain that neurons firing within our brain results in our thought process. And when we are repeatedly in the same situation, the firing pattern of our neurons will be similar and reinforced, thus the reason people react in the same manner when faced with similar situations. This concept suggests that going from negative thoughts to positive thoughts is possible. Our brain has the natural ability to keep unwanted thoughts from spiraling out of control. Simply knowing that a thought is undesirable might be enough to ensure that even when we have unwanted thoughts, they will not increase in strength.

Everyone has imbedded memories they would rather forget, and they may know the triggers that cause them to surface. Sigmund Freud suggested that "humans have a defense mechanism to block unwanted thoughts." If we are not able, or if we have difficulty suppressing our unwanted thoughts, we should at the least attempt to replace them with positive thoughts…there's always plenty to go around!

Sigmund Freud
(May 6, 1856, to September 23, 1939)

Thought Modes

There are several methods of thinking modes, all of which have the common goal to arrive at the best possible solution.

Convergent thinking

This type of thinker focuses in reaching a solution to a problem through the use of logic.

When the shower fails to work, for example, the convergent thinker will immediately call a plumber. The convergent thinker would typically say, "We have a plumbing problem, so let's not mess around with it. Let's call a pro and get it fixed." I have known many convergent-type thinkers who will immediately call a pro without considering any other options. They are either lazy or they don't have the equipment or the experience or knowledge to tackle the problem. They simply call someone who can fix it…problem solved!

Divergent thinking

Divergent thinking is the process of creating multiple ideas or solutions to a problem that we are trying to solve and requires the process of coming up with many different possible solutions. The divergent thinker seems to be the type that thinks just like most of us! He (or she) will consider all options leading to a solution. We have all experienced this type of thinker. They simply love the challenge of trying to resolve problems themselves and without any outside help until absolutely necessary.

For example, should the ceiling fan in the kitchen fail, the divergent thinker will first determine the cause of the problem and then will consider the options to either make the repair himself after reviewing a video on YouTube or consult an experienced friend or call an electrician.

Many of us are capable and technically qualified to make most type of home and auto repairs, whether they involve electrical, plumbing, flooring, construction, plastering, or whatever. On many occasions large drywall area in rooms had to be opened in order to install water pipes, electrical wiring, or coaxial cables, then plaster the holes. One could never tell that a wall repair was made. We always take pride in repairing our own washers, dryers, TVs, and everything else in our home. However, later in life, we begin to realize the dangers in handling power tools, climbing ladders, and the physical efforts required to repair heavy appliances, like refrigerators, washers, and the like, so after the initial diagnose, we would generally call a pro for such repairs. We can then consider our self to be a divergent thinker, not by choice but by necessity.

Lateral thinking

This type of thinking is often referred to as thinking "outside of the box." Solving problems through lateral thinking refers to a person who has the ability to address problems that cannot be arrived at via logical means or the ability to develop original answers to difficult questions.

Macro Thoughts

Macro thoughts in my view further develop our thought process. They are planned thoughts that we experience on a daily basis, such as "I wonder what would happen if I did this or that?" or "I wonder what response I could expect if I write a note to a friend or organization?" I place macro thoughts in the category of major or obvious thoughts that may lead to changing everything, such as the thought of enlisting in the US military. These types of thoughts are typically planned far in advance and generally decided upon after careful and long discussions with those involved or affected in the decision-making process.

We also realize that our final decision may or may not ultimately "work out," but we also realize that the choice made was the best choice at that time. Macro thoughts are the everyday thoughts that require "pros" and "cons" discussions before any final decisions can be considered or implemented. During the process of thinking about writing a note, other micro thoughts may emerge, giving way to further micro thoughts. Some of our macro thoughts may be realized as unnecessary and of no value or perhaps not appropriate and, therefore, need to be deleted while other such thoughts may be accepted and pursued.

Simply viewing objects, such as an automobile or an airplane, can create the thoughts that form or modify our accepted macro thoughts and perhaps an opportunity to scrutinize their values. Upon a mental review, such macro thoughts may either be accepted, rejected, or simply modified. This becomes an ongoing process, but at some point, they may become finalized…at least for that moment.

Micro Thoughts

The acceptance of macro thoughts may influence critical paths along our lives. Not always followed but at least influenced and subject to execution. For example, you may have a macro thought of going on a vacation, and this thought may be followed by more thoughts, such as vacation location, those invited to come along, and our choice of transportation.

Micro thoughts, on the other hand, provide the influence to make alterations. If we decide that driving will be our mode of transportation along our vacation route, we may have macro thoughts to stop for lunch or find a hotel early in the evening. This again may be followed by our selection of motel or the place for lunch or an early dinner. The influences of sudden micro thoughts may drastically or unnoticeably change the course, but we may never know.

The following day will again be filled with micro thoughts, which may alter the time of arrival to our destination, when to stop for car gas, and a host of other unforeseeable events. The forecast for the weather may also have a major impact on our micro thoughts. We may need to take the time to dress accordingly, or we may realize that we need to drive faster slower or to arrive at our hotel earlier or later. Thoughts are the tools we often use in considering and planning a short- or long-term event. Thoughts can also be the product an idea having meaning to "fit" an agenda.

These types of thoughts are created from observing small objects, such as insects or even a tiny grain of sand. For example, while walking on a path, you might step on an ant without realizing it. However, while looking down, you may elect to avoid stepping on the ant, thus generating thoughts, which shape the remainder of your day. At the end of the day, consider all the micro thoughts we experience, which determines the outcome of each day. Would days be otherwise different? We may never know for sure, but it's a one-way street, and we can't travel back or can we ever repeat the same day.

I find it so amusing when I bring babies into my *mental examples* because our relationship with babies have us practicing "thoughts" in so many ways without us even realizing it! We play with them, we talk with them, and we even show them our funny facial expressions. Why? To "hopefully" get a positive reaction in the form of a cute smile or funny sounds. Our reward! But look at it from the baby's perspective. They will react based on how they feel at that moment. If they see you're a good actor, they may reward you with a smile or a remark, otherwise…not. What's my point? This whole process takes us to another level to think about, and we go from there.

"Some thoughts initiate in the form of visions, and vice versa." Einstein is further quoted, "I very rarely think in words at all. A thought comes, and I may try to express in words afterwards."

I find both of these quotes from Einstein to be very powerful in the support of my "thoughts concept."

Albert Einstein
(March 14, 1879, to April 18, 1955)

7

What Is Time?

You walk from your parked car to the grocery store. Are you at the present time? Maybe. You reach the entrance door. It isn't open yet, right? That's in the future. You walk in, and the door closes. The closed door is now in the past and will remain in your past forever. You have now experienced the present, the future, and the past. Time is irrelevant because every moment of your life encompasses present, future, and past. Why do we choose to think that the past is something that happened yesterday or last week or years ago? Why not think the past after the door closed? That, too, may be remembered tomorrow or years from now. Everything we do in every moment is in the present and in the future and in the past all happening at once.

You're standing on the sidewalk watching a car approaching. It passes by you then fades away. How would you evaluate this event? Is there a present? There is a future when the car is approaching, and there is a past after the car fades away, but where is the present? Years from now, you may remember there was an approaching car and there was a fadeaway car, but was there a present?

> *For people like us who believe in physics, know that the distinction between past, present, and future, is only a stubbornly persistent illusion. Time is only an illusion.* (Albert Einstein)

May I have a glass of water? Thank you. Now, just looking at this glass of water would be in the present time, right? The thought of taking a sip would be in the future. A few moments from now, I will take a sip, and then after taking a sip, the sip would be in the past. So after I take a sip, I put the glass aside. Now looking at the glass, one sip was consumed, and that was in the past. Looking at the glass twenty-four hours from now or tomorrow, it's still in the past. All events have, therefore, occurred within moments. Looking at the full glass before taking a sip was the future. After taking a sip became the past. But, in fact, could it all happen at once? What is time?

While sipping, was it the present time? Before the sip was consumed, was that the future? After the sip was consumed, was that the past?

When did the present occur? It didn't occur because while taking the sip, we experienced the future before swallowing and the past after swallowing because water in the glass is always in the future. It didn't occur after consumption because water consumed is always in the past. Was there ever a present? One could argue no because while drinking the water, what's inside the glass is to yet be consumed (future) while what was consumed from the glass was the past. Was there ever a present?

Life consists mainly of the storm of thoughts that is forever flowing through one's head. (Mark Twain)

Mark Twain's quote is simply another powerful tool in support of the "thoughts concept."

Mark Twain
(November 30, 1835, to April 21, 1910)

Many years ago, my close neighbor and friend who worked for a large company asked if I would help him review a stack of résumés one evening in his home. The résumés were not related to my field of engineering. I was simply helping a good friend who was overwhelmed at the time. I was also asked to place the résumés in two stacks, with stack A representing my recommendations.

Of course, I didn't know or even care who the job applicants were or did I ever ask my friend. I was never consulted on my opinions or had I anything to do with deciding on which candidates were hired or considered for further interviews. I was simply asked to place the résumés in two stacks; stack A met the criteria given to me and stack B did not. However, I have since wondered about the important role that I may have played in someone's future, perhaps their career, or even their destiny.

The applicants selected from stack A were to be considered and interviewed for the job or jobs by my very qualified friend and his staff. These candidates may have had to eventually move to another state or country, perhaps marry someone who they never even knew existed prior to applying for the job, have a family that would otherwise not exist, school selections, neighbors, contributions to the community, and so on, all of which would not have otherwise existed. Suppose the qualified applicant in stack A were not selected for the job, everything would have obviously changed for them as well. Suppose, for example, that our father or mother were placed in stack B. Would we exist? Would we be reading this book? Would we be a male, female? Would we have jobs, careers, drive a car, or have friends? Of course not…at least not *us*, but *someone* might! Suppose our father or mother were in stack B. They would perhaps have experienced similar lives but other careers, other children, and, of course, we would obviously not be aware of such.

The Squirrel

I pulled into a parking lot in a small strip mall in my hometown, and while going through some emails, I suddenly noticed this little guy or gal digging a hole in the ground to uncover an acorn he had apparently buried earlier. After he uncovered his acorn, he then hopped on a fence and began to feast on his prize.

Yes, I spent a few moments watching this guy before I decided to take his photo. I then began to think about all the events that were about to follow. Will they all be different had I not parked and spent the time to enjoy my new friend? Of course, they would, but how would they be different, and how could I ever possibly know?

(Photo by the author)

Mahatma Gandhi had this to say about thoughts from his book, *The Story of My Experiments with Truth*: "A man is but the product of his thoughts. What he thinks, he becomes."

Mohandas Mahatma Gandhi
(October 2, 1869, to January 30, 1948)

Yoga

I have found that just one half an hour practicing yoga and fifteen minutes practicing transcendental meditation (TM) on a daily basis was an excellent method to discourage negative thoughts and encourage positive thoughts. It's natural to self-question and evaluate your thoughts, but try to maintain positive thoughts, otherwise you could fall into the trap of the one-legged duck swimming in circles. Be aware that the danger of consequences is a very powerful tool in preventing negative thoughts. When negative thoughts enter your mind, evaluating their real meanings will help to find a positive path to your solutions.

Here's a few examples of what we may be struggling with:

- *"It's important, but I'll think about it later."*
  Did you say think later? This is not a good practice. This is a red flag alerting us to act sooner than later. I always have

quick access to paper and pencil for times when important thoughts pop up. I immediately jot down the important elements of the thought even if just a few key words... otherwise, it's amazing how quickly we forget!

- *"I can't afford it."*
  This thought might just give us a reason to figure out a way to earn more money, sell some of our assets, or even consider a loan.
- *"That would be a total waste of my time."*
  If this is obviously true for us, then "game over." But if we are coping out (and we know if we really are), what may seem to be a waste of time often turns out to be our best choice. We need to carefully evaluate all our pros and cons.

Can We Delete Our Negative Thoughts?

If we look at things from a negative perspective as either being hopeless or beyond our control, they may remain that way and guide us toward undesirable directions. What's that old cliché? If you want to hit a target, aim high. That certainly applies here. It's so easy to fall. As soon as a negative thought comes to mind, drop it and immediately replace it with a positive thought. Just think of something you're comfortable with, a song, a memory, a friend, much like what Joanne used to say to her young patients. You'll be amazed at how habit forming this can become.

Positive Thoughts

Do you recall the recent news media reports about a passenger who fell overboard from a cruise ship? He was in the water for approximately fifteen hours before being rescued by the US Coast Guard. During his television interviews, the young man gave credit for his survival to his *positive thoughts* during the event. He explained that he even sang songs while struggling to stay afloat! In fact, he even changed several undesirable words of the lyrics to assure positive thoughts. He was determined to remove any negative thoughts, which could otherwise cause panic, resulting in a fatal outcome. Yes, positive thoughts…a very powerful tool!

Recently, my wife and I were comfortably sitting in our sunroom enjoying our backyard view, the weather, our coffee, and our conversations. It's so peaceful. While reading the *Cape Cod Times*, I casually mentioned an article about several of our friends that will be performing that night at one of our local establishments. My wife asked to see the newspaper for the details but noticed an announcement about a painting that was being displayed at the Highfield Hall Art Event at our beautifully renovated historic mansion. She suggested that we attend the following day during early afternoon.

I had a positive thought experience in the summer of 1950 when I was seventeen, an experience that I still used to this day. I had built my ham shack in the attic of our two-story home in Newton, which placed me on the third floor. I installed my dipole antenna in my backyard between two tall pine trees. I had previously read of an exercise claiming to strengthen eye muscles, which I subsequently practiced quite often—alternate focusing on a close object then a faraway object.

Although now dwarfed, at that time, the Custom House was the tallest building in Boston, and I could faintly see it from my attic window. I would focus on the window frame then quickly alternate a few inches and focus on the Custom House. I quickly got into the habit of doing this exercise several times a week while in my ham shack, and I credit this exercise to not having to wear eyeglasses; that was until "father time" dictated to do so.

Have you ever experienced severe negative thoughts suddenly overturned to positive thoughts? Our final military basic training event in 1953 was graduation day. I was in the hallway with all my fellow airmen from Flight 2565. It was my turn to enter my drill sergeant's office to learn of the school that I was to attend. I entered his office, gave a sharp salute, and stood at attention, patiently waiting to hear my orders. Since my drill sergeant had previously overheard my strong desire to attend electronics school and of my deepest fear for attending cook school, my drill sergeant firmly said, "Carnevale, your orders are to attend culinary school at McConnell Air Force Base in Kansas."

My heart suddenly stopped. I gave a weak salute and said "Yes, sir," made a slow about-face, and slowly walked back to the door with trembling knees thinking, *How am I going to survive?* As I reached for the doorknob, my drill sergeant shouted, "Carnevale, I'm just kidding, you're assigned to electronic school in Biloxi, Mississippi!"

My heart quickly fell back in place, I made a quick about-face, stood tall, gave a much sharper salute, and firmly said, "Yes, sir. Thank you, sir!"

I made an abrupt about-face, reached for the doorknob, hopped up and down the hallway yelling, "I'm going to electronics school! I'm going to electronics school! I'm going to electronics school!"

All my fellow airmen clapped. They were so happy for me. Many positive thoughts flooded my mind.

My best friend, Al Donkin, was next in line to learn of his orders. Al shortly returned to the hallway with a facial expression I'll never forget. He, too, will attend the same school. Al and I remained in the same outfits up to our discharge in '57 and have been close friends ever since.

Now a military cook school is an excellent thing for those interested in going into that field, and I appreciate that. In fact, I appreciate every aspect of the military. It takes a village, and every position is very important. On initial exams, I scored high in electronics and aviation cadet, so I couldn't understand why I was selected for culinary school. It was quite an experience trying to figure out how to convert all those negative thoughts to positive thoughts. I knew that I could but; I was so thankful that I was selected for electronics school.

Why am I explaining all this? Because to me, it's a thought leading to another event, which shapes our lives. In my wife's view, it was an upcoming art event totally oblivious of the possibilities for any consequences or benefits which may follow. In my view, the notion that simple micro thoughts do not or cannot affect or determine our quality of life or destiny from that point is unrealistic. In fact, micro thoughts, one following another, become the path to which we move throughout our lives. They *are* our moves! Our thoughts may seem to come from nowhere, but in my view, they can be triggered by any tangible or intangible source. Then once triggered, actions or events generally follow.

While I was living alone in Lakeville, Connecticut, in 1985, positive thoughts led me to consider attending a professional singles club. Being very shy, it took a lot to motivate me to follow through. I did, however, and meanwhile, Joanne apparently felt the same five years after her husband passed away. We met at the club, and I haven't taken my eyes and focus away from Joanne ever since. We have been happily married since 1987.

It's so gratifying to have positive thoughts. On two separate occasions last week, Joanne and I were running a little late on our way to a trip and on our way to a meeting. On the first event, we were several miles away from home when Joanne realized that she forgot something. Realizing that things happen for a reason, we drove back home to get that something. The trip turned out wonderful, and we knew that it would. Similarly, on the second event, after driving several miles from home, I realized that I forgot something, so we drove back home to get it. Again, realizing that things happen for a reason, we arrived at the meeting, all went well, and we had a wonderful day. Difficult as it might be at times when such a situation occurs, it's so gratifying to know that things will work out.

We have all experienced such delays much too often, but my hope is that we understand it is what it is and we simply make necessary adjustments along the way. I came across the following quote, which falls directly in line with positive thinking, "Sometimes God holds you back temporary until the road is safe and clear to continue." Be thankful for the stall.

Are We Disappointed?

I had a difficult time selecting the right title for this topic. I could have very well picked upset, discouraged, angry, or many other synonyms, but let's group them all together for this topic. Of course, we experience all these and many times over. Who wouldn't be discouraged or whatever if our child didn't make the soccer team? It's only natural. But my point in this topic is not to allow these bad moments to linger or dwell. Don't look for ways to blame other individuals or to blame "the system." Short-lived the moment and realize "it is what it is" and move on.

The world continues to spin, and tomorrow will come. Use our energy to think of ways to resolve these issues. Look for alternatives. We may conclude it was meant to be and better outcomes are on the horizon. Days, weeks, or months later, when things do work out, let's not forget to look back at what seemed to be the end of the world and reward ourselves for our patience and ability to think positively.

Our world is full of negative and positive situation, and we need to know about both types. However, our focus on positive thoughts is not only healthy but resonates on those around us, our families, and our careers. We tend to shy away from those who constantly complain, and we gravitate toward those with happy and productive positive thoughts.

Yes, we have a choice: either live in a climate of hate and destruction or in a climate of understanding and love. There's a lot of good people in our world, people who feel a need to help and do something about it. Such people always have a positive outlook and are drawn into our circle. Welcome, you provide and enhance our positive thoughts.

> *How you think about a problem is more important than the problem itself, so always think positively.* (Dr. Norman Vincent Peale)

After we decided to retire on Cape Cod, we checked out many homes until we found our "dream" home. We returned to Connecticut to think it over. A few days later, we decided to make a deposit only to discover our dream home was sold. Imagine our disappointment? We immediately thought, *Let's go back to Cape Cod to find another home. A better home.* We did and have since been very pleased that the house, which we failed to make a deposit, was sold. Yes, things do work out for the better. I have a frown when I hear people refer to their home as a house. "I recently had my house painted." In my view, a house is something built from materials, whereas a home is something built from love as in the cliché "Home is where the heart is."

What's an Angel?

You could ask this question to many people, and the response received would probably vary with most answering, "I don't really know." Before my retirement, my response may have been similar as I had no conclusive answer. I could not clearly define what an angel is. But after retirement, it slowly began to sink in. An angel was clear in my mind, perfect in every way. I think age helps people to think more deeply, separates the good from the not so good, and allows common sense and wisdom to take over.

Back in the late 1990s, we were on our way to Vermont for a ski adventure getaway trip. Before arriving to our cabin, we saw a car that appeared to be stuck in a mud-and-snow mix. The engine was screeching while one of the back wheels was burning rubber, and two young girls seemed desperate. We pulled over to observe the situation. Then we searched for tree branches. We snapped the branches into working lengths and placed several in the muddy trench made by the wheel. We also placed branches on the ground to serve as a pavement once the wheel drove out of the trench.

I asked the girls to get back in their car and try to drive off as Joanne and I pushed from the back of the car. We were sure to be careful not to get in the way of the branches, possibly being propelled by the spinning wheels. They started the engine, put the gear into drive, and stepped on the gas pedal. The wheel came out of the trench and onto the makeshift pavement. The design worked perfectly! However, they immediately stopped to thank us, and their car rolled back into the trench. No problem, we know the design works, so let's rebuild.

Before their second attempt, I told them that once they get out of the trench, they just keep accelerating and do not stop. "We will say our goodbyes now." They started the engine, placed the gear into drive, stepped on the gas pedal, pull out of the trench, and sounded their horn while driving out of sight. What a beautiful feeling we had in the joy of knowing we helped someone. Medication could never give such a feeling. It comes only from helping someone in need or in distress.

After Joanne's brother-in-law passed away in Newark, California, Joanne was asked to make the trip to Newark to meet with our attorney and settle the estate. On our return home, we were sitting at the gate waiting for our flight back to Boston. Several flight delays caused an anxiety, which we were dealing with. We happened to be sitting very close to the American Airlines Admiral Club when suddenly the club door opened; a representative approached and addressed me by my name. The representative explained that she had arranged a prepaid taxi to drive us to the San Francisco airport and a boarding pass for a flight to Boston. Our luggage was loaded into the taxi, and the driver took us directly to the airport. Upon arrival, we entered the gate, boarded the aircraft, and enjoyed the remainder of our trip. The entire experience occurred quickly. However, after reality set in, I explained to Joanne how incredible this experience was as my membership with the American Airlines Admiral Club had expired well over fifteen years ago. Why did the AA representative even care or know where or who I was? And why would she even provide a boarding pass and prepaid taxi? These are questions we never found answers to. Our only possible conclusion was the help of an angel.

One of the most dramatic experiences I have ever had was during a trip to a marketing firm in Michigan to discuss my recent patent pending invention. The date was January 23, 2002. I left Cape Cod and stopped at a hotel on Interstate 80 near Scranton, Pennsylvania. After a good breakfast the following morning and after driving for half an hour, I developed a cold sweat, blurry vision, and lightheadedness. I apparently passed out while driving approximately seventy miles an hour. I vividly recall having a smiling expression on my face and thinking about crashing into a viaduct. I was waiting for this to happen as I felt it was inevitable. I could hear and feel my 2009 Prius run over shrubs but didn't know at the time that I was running over the shoulder off the highway.

My Prius came to a quiet and safe stop only a few feet short of a metal black-and-yellow striped end cap roadside barrier. I slowly regained consciousness and focused around the area; I was uncertain whether my car was damaged or if I was injured. After turning off the engine, I slowly open the door and casually walked around my Prius to assess any damages then returned to the driver's seat and drove off. I was totally overwhelmed that such as incident could result in a perfect landing.

After I arrived at my destination, I called Joanne, and she advised that I go to the nearest hospital. I checked into the hospital and was kept overnight. All tests were negative. After my meeting and after driving home to Cape Cod, I discovered several small twigs still wedged in the undercarriage of my Prius. I remove the twigs then placed them into a frame as a reminder of this miraculous experience.

Twigs found in my Prius undercarriage
(Photo by the author)

Since that time, I have attempted to recreate this situation many times, driving at seventy miles an hour on various interstates then letting go of the wheel and gas pedal to see what would happen.

I was not surprised to find that on each experiment, my Prius either veered to the left or to the right, and at each time, I had to quickly grab the steering wheel to avoid a self-created accident. Of the many attempts, my Prius never even came close to a safe stop or any kind of stop. Yes, I had to have been "carried" to safety.

When things go wrong

Something good will come out of it. But what does that mean? What if nothing good comes of it? And how long shall we wait? Well, I believe we may never know because the "something good" may not affect us. Why should it always affect us directly? Could it affect someone else? Of course! Are we rationalizing? I believe that if not us, then something or someone! Should we think that a bad situation may somehow or eventually benefit us? Yes, but perhaps not directly. Let's think positively. Let's exercise our faith and believe that some good will come of it even if just a little. The power of prayer should not be challenged.

Our ski adventure was fun, and on our trip back to Connecticut, we discussed the girls that were in distress and how wonderful it was to be there at the right time to help them. Yes, angels are wingless individuals on Earth. They are you, and they are me. They are us, and they are those who suddenly realize the need or desire to help those in distress. We have all experienced someone helping us when we are in need. That, in my view, is exactly what angels are!

I was driving back to my home on Cape Cod in November of 2019 after a long weekly jam session in Quincy, Massachusetts. The trip was about an hour and a half. While driving on the interstate about 1:30 AM, I noticed a young girl desperately waving her arms in an attempt to get a motorist's attention. She was far back from the shoulder, and it was difficult to see her. However, for some reason, I was able to see her. I immediately pulled over, got out of my car, and asked if she was all right. She said yes and then said she was very cold and wanted to call her dad in New Jersey. I put my western denim jacket over her shoulders. I was dressed in my white Stetson hat, white western shirt, dungaree, and cowboy boots.

21

Knowing that she may not trust me, I gave her my car keys as I remained a distance from my car. I told her to get into my car, start the engine, and turn on the heat. The doors will lock automatically. My phone is on the passenger seat, and she could call her dad. She later stepped out of my car, thanked me, and we both waited for her dad. While waiting, I took several photos of her totally wrecked car. The brush and the swamp areas were extreme. My white shirt was beyond cleaning or repair, and my dungarees and boots were wet, cold, and dirty. Getting home was of no concern as well as any fear or danger in this dark, wooded area.

So what was the concern? Her safety, her knowing that someone is there to help, someone who cares, someone who won't leave her until knowing she is in trusted hands. But who was that someone? Was it me? I think it was someone beyond me. Have I described an angel? Is it selfish, self-centered, or egotistical to even consider yourself an angel? No, I don't think so. I believe that being an angel means to be humble, to want to help others in need, and to be caring and concerned about others. There's nothing selfish about wanting to help.

The author helping a motorist in distress.
(Photo by the author)

Saving Lives

When I enlisted in the US Air Force in 1953, I recall my drill sergeant explaining, "You will all soon have responsibilities." I wasn't quite sure just what he meant by that at the time, but during my military career, I found out exactly what he meant. We are either directly or indirectly responsible for all our decisions and our actions. I was educated in electronics while at Keesler AFB in Biloxi, Mississippi, then assigned as a crew chief on an F-86 flight simulator in the famed Eddie Rickenbacker's 94th Fighter Interceptor Squadron "Hat in the Ring" squadron.

Capt. Eddie Rickenbacker, 94th Aero Squadron
(October 8, 1890 to July 23, 1973)

Willard Marriott had this to say, *"View the problem as an opportunity to grow."*

Willard "Bill" Marriott
(September 17, 1900, to August 13, 1985)

In the spring of 1955 about 2:00 AM, I was driving back to Selfridge Air Force Base in Michigan where I was stationed. The narrow road had no traffic at that hour, and no one was in sight. I saw what appeared to be two bright lights placed vertically one above the other. As I drove closer, it was an automobile on its side. I pulled over to the side of the road and called QRRR on my ham mobile rig (QRRR was the emergency call back in the '50s).

Some hams continually monitor their receivers on a scan, and fortunately, a ham quickly responded. I explained the situation and asked for police and ambulance. Sitting on the ground by their car was a man and a woman in their sixties.

The man was unconscious with a quarter-size hole in the outer part of his left arm at his bicep. The woman was screaming for help while punching and scratching at me. Blood was pouring out from the hole in his bicep, so I took my handkerchief and made a tourniquet above the hole to stop the bleeding all the while protecting myself from the frantic woman. His vitals seemed to be normal as the woman and I waited about ten long minutes before the police and ambulance arrived. After the ambulance drove away, the police called for a tow truck to remove the damaged car. During this time, my 1948 Nash Rambler rolled from the side of the road into a deep drain ditch. The tow driver was kind enough to pull me out free of charge as he could tell I was a GI.

By this time, it was close to 3:00 AM, and I was the last one to leave the scene. After I stopped at an intersection traffic light, the police officers from the accident pulled up next to my car, and one said, "Hey, thanks for what you did, soldier. Sorry you lost a good handkerchief."

In the summer of 1960, we moved into our first newly built home in Michigan. It was across from acres of grassy fields with several large trees. I was wearing slippers while mowing my small front lawn when suddenly I could faintly hear a voice crying out for help. I immediately ran across the field. My slippers fell off. Now running barefoot over tall grass and brush, I approached the tree where the crying came from. It was a child about forty feet up the tree with his right foot wedged between the trunk and a branch forming a Y. I climbed the tree, took hold of the branch, and told the child to lift his foot off the joint on the count of three. The poor child was so frightened that he climbed down and quickly ran out of sight back to his distant home. I can only imagine the outcome had I not heard his cry for help. My thoughts, leading to mowing the lawn, put me at the right place at the right time.

The year was 2017, and I was attending my seventh annual pedal steel guitar seminar in St. Louis, Missouri. I approached the elevator to go down to the seminar when I discovered a man's wallet on the floor at the entrance to the elevator. I picked up the wallet, went down the elevator, and into the seminar room. I asked for an announcement over the PA for a lost wallet, but no one came forward. I approached the desk, but no one had inquired about a lost wallet. The desk contacted security, but when security arrived, they asked for the wallet and explained they would attempt to contact the owner. In all due respect, I told the security officer that I would prefer to hold onto the wallet and personally give it to the owner.

My second attempt on the PA did not result in anyone coming forward to claim the wallet. I continued checking at the desk. I was determined to spend the remainder of the day going without meals and missing seminars until I locate the owner on the wallet. I opened the wallet. There was a bundle of bills of which I didn't even bother to count as the amount was of no concern to me. The driver's license showed that Mr. X was from Arizona. I immediately thought how difficult it would be for Mr. X to board his aircraft, not to mention all the other problems and inconveniences in replacing the driver's license, Social Security card, etc., etc.

Later that afternoon while still roaming the lobby, the halls, the seminar room, and more announcements on the PA, I saw a security guard with a middle-aged man and woman walking briskly down the hallway, toward me. I asked the man for his name and address. All matched his driver's license including the photo.

They were both so happy to see me and explained the difficulties they would have when returning to Arizona without proof of identification. The woman gave me a big hug and began crying. The man asked me to keep all the money in the wallet, but I refused. I told them I didn't even count the money, had no idea how much was in the wallet, nor did I even care. I told them I was deeply satisfied to have located them and able to directly return their wallet. They walked away overjoyed.

As time passed, I couldn't help thinking how I would have felt had I been the one who lost my wallet. And after retrieving my wallet in a similar manner, I would want to know the individual who found it and be thankful for his or her dedicated efforts to return it. But after rethinking the situation, there is no real good reason for the

Arizonians to know me or get in touch with me, as well as there is no good reason for me to ever contact them. It was simply a situation that left the three of us overjoyed. And that was more than enough!

Positive Strokes

This is always an interesting topic. We all like positive strokes. Not only do they imply gratitude for us, but they also provide confidence for us. We feel better and walk away thinking, *I didn't realize that anyone cared or was even appreciative of my efforts.* In fact, it's nice knowing that someone is even aware. Positive strokes allow you to become a better person and "guides" your thoughts in more ways than we ever imagined or considered.

Everyone Has the Best Barber

I have the best pastor! Consider the multitude of thoughts we acquire after listening to an inspiring sermon. Thoughts that could otherwise move us in different directions. How many of us feel that a good deed is eminent after hearing a good sermon.

Can We Control Our Destinies?

In my opinion, yes, we can control our destinies but indirectly! How? Many thoughts flash passed us uncontrollably because they randomly happen anywhere and at any time. However, if we think positively and spiritually, we tend to blank out our undesirable thoughts.

During my life, I have made a practice (now a habit) to always pray for encouragement and guidance before entering a facility to give a talk or a lecture, a musical jams session, and musical gigs. In fact, any kind of event. I find that filling my mind with positive thoughts places me in the path for success. Does it work all the time? Yes and no. However, when it doesn't work, I still give thanks because I know the message of failure always provides a great opportunity for me to evaluate my flaws, which leads to further opportunities for corrections. I have learned that failure equals opportunities.

More recently, I thought I would do something about a clicking noise in one of the hinges on a kitchen cupboard door. I oiled the hinge as I do for every hinge and moving parts in my home every year, but this time, it didn't get rid of the clicking noise. After close investigation, I discovered a broken part in the hinge. I removed the hinge and decided to buy a replacement at the Home Depot.

My first stop was to pick up some unrelated items opposite of the direction to Home Depot. The local Aubuchon Hardware store was close by, so I decided to see if they would have a replacement hinge. A sales associate greeted and guided me to the cupboard hinge area. I spent some time looking at all the hinges, but nothing was close. I begin to leave the store thinking about the twenty-five-mile trip to our local Home Depot.

However, a different sales associate was just finishing with a customer conversation with his customer as I walked past him. The timing was perfect. He asked if I found what I was looking for. I was going to reply yes just to avoid further discussions, but for some unknown reason, I showed him my defective hinge, and he immediately took me to a different area of the store where cabinet hinges were displayed. I explained that I couldn't find a replacement hinge. He found a hinge that perfectly matched my hinge, then I left the store and headed for home. On my way home, I thought of all the what-ifs. What if I viewed the first hinges for a shorter or longer time? I would not have walked past the salesman at the exact time he ended the conversation with his customer.

These situations happen to all of us on a daily basis, but how many of us care or even think about the what-ifs? I do because I believe this coincidental, ironic situation happens for a reason. These situations determine our next move.

Another similar incident occurred while driving around Memphis, Tennessee, looking for the Grace Mansion. I was in Memphis to give a lecture and had plenty of time to look around after breakfast. I asked the waitress for directions to Grace Mansion, and after following her directions, I realized something was wrong, so I asked another local for directions. His directions didn't work either. I asked a third, and bingo, it took me directly to Grace Mansion.

You can imagine how many thoughts and what-ifs passed through my mind! My message is that we learn to realize that things happen for a reason although along the way we may get discouraged, disappointed, angry, or disturbed. But it always works out. And if it doesn't work out, guess what? It still works out because what is meant to be is meant to be…it is what it is.

Chapter 2

Traveling Is Involved

Introduction

Most of us know that the individual who reviews our résumés and conducts our interviews, may determine whether we will be hired or not. If we are hired, we're overjoyed, but we never actually stop to think about the alternatives, which in itself is endless in "thoughts." Hired for the job opens a whole new world for us as well as not being hired. In the latter, would we continue with our existing jobs with thoughts of what could have been? Or could we rationalize and use our positive thoughts to consider the new job may have required excessive traveling or a transfer at a later date to some undesirable location? The third thought or option could be to accept the outcome, knowing "things will work out for the best," meaning a new window for creating positive thoughts toward future opportunities.

Requesting a Transfer

A military individual applying for duty in Germany, for example, may submit his or her request for a transfer. However, the military individual evaluating the transfer application may have a need for qualified military personnel elsewhere, or perhaps the evaluator may decide to call it a day and make his decision on the next day. But during the following day, schedules may have changed, and there may suddenly be a need for military personnel in Japan, for example, and you may be the one selected for duty in Japan without ever realizing that the decision in this situation is nothing more than a continuation in *shaping* the next phase of our future, our destinies, and everything in between! Had we been assigned to Germany for our duty as we had initially requested, then consider the many possibilities of the friends we may have made, or perhaps getting married to someone in Germany and raising our family.

Now let's think about the similar possibilities of our "would-be" duties in Japan. Similar situations may have taken place. We may have married and started our new family and so on. However, our children would not have even existed had we transferred to Germany and vice versa. Our children's lives would be entirely lived without them realizing that it could not have been at all, and they would not know those who they now know or they would not become who they are…in fact, there wouldn't even be a "they"!

Do we realize the potential impact the many series of events that could follow and may have on our destinies but still take this very lightly? And perhaps the only things that comes to our mind at the time is that "we're going to Germany"? Or the amazing people and sites we would have experienced? Or the impact of "we're going to Japan"? Similar thoughts? Yes, but without the realization that our children could have been either born in Germany or in Japan. Life would exist for one and not for the other and vice versa! Although this scenario may be typical to many of us, we go about or daily lives without considering the simple thoughts leading to decisions made by others that has placed us where we are, and that has made us who we are.

The Broken Airplane

We further understand that when we are in an airplane and should it develop a mechanical malfunction, the pilot may need to immediately land at a different airport. We may think, *I wish I had taken a different flight*. But look at those possibilities. Had you taken a different flight, the current situation would not have existed for you. And although that may be true since you did take the aircraft which later developed a malfunction, that event is going to guide the rest of your life to your eventual destiny, and that is what one's life is all about: circumstances that come about unexpectedly or unintentionally.

But take the situation with the aircraft that developed a malfunction and had to land at a different airport. Of course, this changes our entire lives. Things may happen while we're at that different airport that is going to affect, change, or delay other situations in our lives of which we would otherwise be oblivious. Had we been on a different flight to begin with, we'd have met different people, make different types of phone calls, etc. All of which guides our lives and, hence, our destinies.

We need to learn not to be disappointed or upset due to such events. Everything happens for a reason, and the reasons I believe, are meant to guide and shape our lives. With this in mind, we learn to accept the "bad with the good" as we move forward.

What About Children?

How do you prevent children from becoming upset or disappointed? Yes, it's very difficult, but consider these situations as great opportunities to show firsthand how you handle these events. We don't fabricate these undesirable situations, but when we are faced with them, we should take advantage of the opportunities. Imagine a major league baseball team losing in the home park by a score of, let's say, 12 to 3 in the bottom of the ninth inning only to end up winning the game! During the game, it was a situation where the home team did not want to be in, but after the game was over, they were overjoyed to have had the opportunity to show their fans and the sports world what they are really made of!

Consider the stock market and how we hate to see the Dow take a severe tumble. But those who take advantage of such an opportunity to further invest usually end up on top. In fact, they even plan for the next *big* opportunity!

Am I Too Late for This Accident?

While approaching an auto accident at an intersection, or on the highway, how often have we thought, *Wow, one or two more sec-*

onds later and that could have been me in that accident? Well, perhaps earlier that day when you backed away from your driveway and you suddenly realized that you had forgotten something and understandably became upset or even angry for having to turn back for that "something," well, if you had not forgotten that something, it could very well have been *you* in that auto accident! Understanding that possibility, there should be no reason to have been disturbed about going back to get anything you may have forgotten without first realizing "what could have resulted otherwise." Such a delay could have prevented an accident. A blessing in disguise?

Planning for an event

Another example is when we find ourselves in a situation where we get together with several neighbors or friends and plan to go out for dinner and deciding on which restaurant to honor. Our final decision could have also resulted in or prevented an auto accident or forgetting your gas level and run out of gas or a multitude of other possibilities. In different scenarios where we successfully arrive at our destination after traveling to visit someone, or perhaps driving to a specific event and getting there safely, had any thoughts interrupted our mind path for just one moment, the results could have been much different. We may have decided to go elsewhere, and several other situations could have easily developed. We may have experienced this in the past. Many times, while driving on familiar routes, we may suddenly decide to take different roads. Why? Perhaps for a change of scenery. But think of all the possible outcomes that could have resulted from these sudden thoughts.

Thoughts That Made a Career

I vividly recall that in the summer of 1947, when I turned fourteen years old, an incident occurred, which not only sparked my fascinating career, but also taught me one of the most important lessons in my life. My sister Gina was thumbing through a *Saturday Evening Post* magazine one afternoon while chatting with my brother. She just happened to come across an item in the magazine that gave her the thought about going shopping. Several hours later, my sister and brother returned from shopping, and while I was in the bathroom, I heard my sister calling, "Hey, Ben, we have a surprise for you." I opened the door just enough to take their gift and to say "Thank you."

Hugo Gernsback

Their gift to me was a *Radio Craft* magazine by Hugo Gernsback, the father of science fiction (who was coined with that term in 1929). Although I was very thankful for their gift, I was somewhat disappointed because I wasn't really interested in radio or electronics. Then while flipping through the boring pages, and before putting the magazine down to rest, I happen to spot a table of the Morse code on one of the pages. My eyes lit up...I was absolutely fascinated! The Morse code for all the letters from A to Z, for all the numbers from 1 to 10, and all the common punctuations. Wow!

Hugo Gernsback, "The Father of Science Fiction"
(August 16, 1886, to August 19, 1967)

While still in the bathroom, I studied and memorized the entire Morse code table within a ten-minute period! I eventually became an amateur radio operator (ham) later in life, and I have never forgotten the Morse code to this day. This event was responsible for my electronics education and long, exciting electronics career.

Dr. Wernher von Braun

I was an electronics supervisor in the US Air Force Research and Development on one of the first computers, electronics tech on developing the first printed circuit boards, and on the Jupiter-C and the Redstone missile that launched the first American, Alan Shepard Jr., into space on May 5, 1961, under the Mercury-Redstone Missile-3 program.

Launch of the Mercury-Redstone-3
(Photo courtesy of NASA)

I was part of the electrical engineering team responsible for designing, building, and testing all the electronics located inside the white-and-black stripe section under the top space capsule.

Dr. Wernher von Braun, Redstone Missile
(March 23, 1912, to June 16, 1977)

Dr. Armand Hammer

The many years I worked with Occidental Petroleum, Dr. Hammer's group was exceptional and fascinating. I was involved with the preliminary design and development of DC power systems where I met the most talented and interesting engineers and physicists during my career. Positive thoughts were in constant flow.

Dr. Armand Hammer, Occidental Petroleum
(May 21, 1898, to December 10, 1990)
Author: FDR Presidential Library & Museum.
This photo is subject to a Creative Commons License
https://creativecommons.org/licenses/by/2.0/deed.en
No changes were made to this photo.

My career in electronics would not have existed had my sister not pursued the thought which prompted her to go shopping that afternoon. None of this would have happened had she not by chance come across the *Radio Craft* magazine on the magazine shelf. All these events, and all these thoughts, have such an unexpected impact on our lives. The lesson that I learned from this experience was *if you really want to learn something bad enough, and I mean really bad enough, you* will *learn it!*

Gina was born in Catanzaro, Italy, in 1923 and migrated to the United States with our parents in 1930 at the age of seven. She was later educated in fashion design, and her "thoughts" led her to a long and fascinating profession.

Gina
(May 25, 1923 to January 5, 2007)

One of Gina's many designs from the late 1940s

Are We Part of the Solution?

We have all experienced those standing on street corners and highway intersections holding up signs asking for monetary donations. Although many reasons are stated on these signs for our "generous donations," I learned many years ago that money may just be the "evil cause" that placed these unfortunate people under such situations in the first place. My approach to their requests has always been to first ask if they are hungry. On several occasions, the responses that I received was that of anger, which caused me to politely drive away. However, in situations when "yes, I am hungry" was the response, I would take their food order, drive to the closest fast-food chain, then return with the goods…and, yes, I would always throw in a monitory donation in appreciation for their humble honesty.

Who knows how the many thoughts generated by this simple exchange of dialogue and trust could influence our next as well as our future paths and theirs, I might add. They demonstrated a humble request (a very difficult thing to do) while demonstrating trust and a sincere need for help. Are there other ways to handle these types of scenarios? Of course, there are, and we get to choose how we respond. However, pause now to consider the type and quality of your thoughts going forward.

Thoughts and Religion

Ask and thou shall receive, but how does God answer our requests? How does He communicate with us? These are both good questions; unfortunately, some believe He doesn't answer us while others believe He does. But how does He answer us? Here are my views on the matter: when asking our Creator for answers to our needs or for guidance with our difficult problems or decisions, will we know where to search for His answers or guidance? Will we receive some sort of sign or perhaps a "thought"? Remember, our Creator also gave us the ability to know right from wrong…and *there* could be our answers. We typically consider the pros and cons when making a decision. The answers may not always be what we expect or what we want to hear, but they will be the right choice. It's called "faith," and those that don't have it may not understand.

Years ago, a friend asked what the purpose of life was. Why am I here? I turned the question around and I asked, "What is your answer? Why do you think you are here? What is the purpose of you being here?" My friend replied, "To enjoy life, to enjoy every moment, to travel, meet people, party, and just have a good time." I said, "Well, that's wonderful, but you know the real purpose for us being here and the reason for our existence. Have you ever seen a rainbow, a puppy, a baby, the Milky Way?" My friend got the idea quickly. In my opinion, we're here to enjoy everything that God has given us and to care and love one another. The best things are possible and free of charge.

After God built Earth, sky, and the entire universe; it was so good that He put us here on Earth to enjoy His creations. Trees, scenery, lakes, oceans, mountains, star, planets, moon…the universe! That's the whole purpose of us being on this Earth. I guess my friend felt that the purpose of his life on Earth was to enjoy it to its fullest, enjoy what life has to offer, and to simply take advantage of the once-in-a-lifetime opportunity. I understand that, and I get it, but he said nothing about the beauty of God's creations. I'm not saying that nature is solely for our existence and our happiness, but I am saying that we may want to have a few celebrations now and then, like travel, etc.

But we also need to realize that the best things in life have already been given to us…to all of us and free of charge. Everyone can afford them! As far as the purpose of us being here…it's a matter of sharing our happiness from our personal wants and needs with the happiness from the many gifts given to us. I do believe that most of us realize that our purpose of being here on Earth is to enjoy the many gifts given to us by God and to enjoy our personal needs and wants in the amount of moderation as to how and where we find our happiness. It's fifty-fifty!

1 Timothy 6:17–19 and Ecclesiastes 3:11–13

On July 9, 2023, Pastor Jim substituted for our Pastor Jonathan and gave this inspirational sermon referencing the book of Genesis chapter 24. This biblical passage explains that after Abraham's wife died, he asked his oldest servant to search for a wife for his son Isaac. Upon searching, the servant came across Rebekah who immediately offered to draw well water for the weary servant and for his ten tired camels. The servant could see the kindness in Rebekah and asked her to be the wife of Abraham's son Isaac. Rebekah agreed. The servant did not look at Rebekah's appearance or her external features, only at her internal heart and spirit.

This passage tells us that Rebekah was simply full of positive thoughts such that her only desire was to offer help and support to those in need. Throughout my life, I made it a sincere practice to pray every day as well as every night before bedtime, and I always say, "Thank you, Lord, for my wisdom, my knowledge, and my patience." I pray for all my friends and my relatives, and I request a very special job as an angel to help people and animals in their time of need. I would really love that!

Pledge

One of the many inspiring sermons given by my pastor entitled "A Pledge to Encourage Positive Thoughts and Discourage Negative Thoughts" was among his best. I felt this sermon was well in support of my thoughts concept and worth watching again. The sermon by Reverend Johnathan Drury was recorded at the First Congregational Church of Falmouth on March 12, 2023, and is available online on the Church website.

Matthew 20:1–16

This is one of my favorite passages in the Bible. To me, it explains the essence of fairness. Ask many, and 100 percent will say they are fair to everyone including their children. For it's the normal response. However, in reality, children need to be treated accordingly. Of course, when taking them out for ice cream, you treat them all evenly and fairly. However, when it comes to disciplining them, they need to be dealt with individually as some children require only a scolding. I think this passage tells me that we lost something somewhere along the way. So what is fair to the subordinate fairness is to be treated as others are treated; unless others are being treated unfairly, then there is no need for complaint. To the leader, fairness is making an offer which once accepted is considered a fair agreement by both parties. This passage was given by lay reader Olivia White at the First Congregational Church of Falmouth on October 1, 2023, and is available online on the Church website.

Obstacles

Forgot where you put your car keys? Did you painfully stub your toe? Consider these as opportunities and not as things to get disturbed or upset about. Hard, I know! But, yes, these things do happen and, in many instances, too often. For example, I recently started out one morning by realizing that I didn't have my smart car key with me while I was attempting to start my hybrid. I searched everywhere around my home, but wait, I can't go anywhere anyway without my travel mug filled with coffee. Yet another delay.

My neighbor was walking with her dog one afternoon, and when they crossed at the end of my driveway, I just had to jump out of my car to say hello and play with one of my best four-legged friends Michaela, a super adorable and cute brown and white female King Charles spaniel. So at the end of the day, I dwelled on the number of delays as I often do to have taken about forty-five minutes. That's a big wow to me because I immediately thought about the events I missed caused by these delays, which could have resulted in either good or bad situations…I will never know.

The pinball machine from the beginning of its playful journey to its final "game over" encounters many obstacles of which results in either rewards or penalties. This analogy could be applied not only to humans but to nature as well.

While watching the news on TV one night, the program reported that a car had crashed through the side of a house in my state of Massachusetts. During an interview with a television reporter, the homeowner explained that he was sitting in his living room and for some unexplained reason, suddenly decided to get up to get something from his bedroom. Moments later a car slammed through his living room. Again, typical of thoughts and what-ifs.

Quite often while driving on local roads, we may feel like turning on the radio to listen to some good ole time music to put some of those positive thoughts in our minds. But I find that the type of music today just doesn't seem to accomplish that, so I tune around the dial both on the AM and FM bands to find a station that play songs from yesteryear. I usually find such a station, and it brings a smile to my face every time. Good music and good memories develops great thoughts.

I always look forward to going for a long walk or a drive by the ocean here on Cape Cod to watch the sky touch the ocean and the ocean surf touch the sand. Such beautiful moments open my mind to positive thoughts.

Here are some "thought" quotes that are among my favorite.

Do we need friends?

Of course, we do! Friends support and enhance our positive thinking. Although some may not, we cannot allow such individuals to "ruin our day" or better yet "our agenda." Surrounding ourselves with good friends is key. I have found such friends in all my travels, in particular, my childhood, my church, my careers, and especially my music gigs and jam sessions.

Among my favorite is my long-term (over a decade) song-circle jam sessions. I have found that music is one of the best activities for positive thinking. It's a magnet for the planning, playing, friendships, fun, camaraderie, and the togetherness…it just can't get any better.

Partial members of our "Musical family"
Left to right: Michael No. 2 Correira, Richard Latimer, Curtis Bakal,
Frank Carotenuto, Wayne Stuck, Carol Bednarz, David Knaack,
Kyah Faria, Ralph Carlson, Ben Carnevale, Ursula Boyce, Dan
"Lefty" Warncke, Laura Higgins, Bob Higgins, Norah Connelly,
Michael No. 1 Shea, Al Tomek, Doug Correllus, and Jeff Brown

Quotes on Thoughts

"A positive attitude causes a chain reaction of positive thoughts, events, and outcomes. It is a catalyst, and it sparks extraordinary results" (Wade Boggs, Boston Red Sox, third baseman).

Wade Boggs
(June 15, 1958 to present)
Author: Ted Straub. This photo is subject to a Creative Commons License
https://creativecommons.org/licenses/by-sa/2.0/deed.en
No changes were made to this photo.
Photo for identification purposes only.
Mr. Boggs has not endorsed or participated
in the publication of this book.

"The truth is that there is no actual stress or anxiety in the world; it's your thoughts that create these false beliefs. You can't package stress, touch it, or see it. There are only people engaged in stressful thinking" (Wayne Dyer, Author).

"You are today where your thoughts have brought you; you will be tomorrow where your thoughts take you" (Wayne Dyer, Author).

"If you realized how powerful your thoughts are, you would never think a negative thought" (James Allen, Writer).

"What matters is to live in the present, live now, for every moment is now. It is your thoughts and acts of the moment that create your future. The outline of your future path already exists, for you created its pattern by your past" (Peace Pilgrim, Activist).

"It is your thoughts and acts of the moment, that create your future" (Sai Baba, Spiritual Leader).

"Remember that stress doesn't come from what's going on in your life. It comes from your thoughts about what's going on in your life" (Andrew J. Bernstein, Philosopher).

"When the negative thoughts come, and they will; they come to all of us. It's not enough to just not dwell on it. You've got to replace it with a positive thought" (Joel Osteen, Theologist).

"Once you replace negative thoughts with positive ones, you'll start having positive results" Willie Nelson, Musician/Songwriter).

Willie Nelson
(April 30, 1933 to present)
Photo for identification purposes only. Mr. Nelson has not endorsed or participated in the publication of this book.

"Being aware that the danger of consequences is a very powerful tool in preventing negative thoughts" (Confucius).

"The more man meditates upon good thoughts, the better will be his world and the world at large" (Confucius).

Removing Stress

I read a report many years ago that I thought was very interesting. The report was in reference to why more people have heart attacks after midnight. It went on to say that it was not because we eat a lot late at night or that our blood pressure is too high or we're overweight or because we're not getting sufficient exercise or not because of sleep apnea. It was because we are more stressed out at night. Our body releases a ton of stress hormones late in the evening.

Then if we are stressed out, we experience the worst symptoms during this time, like dizziness, tingling of the hands, cold and sweaty hands or feet, rapid heart rate, and even chest pains. We actually experience many of these symptoms late at night rather than any other time of the day. When our heart rate goes up, our heart becomes incapable of pumping blood efficiently. We pile up a lot of our emotions, like anxiety, anger, and stress, which circulate throughout our body.

Therefore, if we are too stressed, our body will release these undesirably emotions all at one time. Since reading this report, it reinforced my "thoughts concept" in which I feel that thinking about something pleasant before falling asleep—such as a vacation trip, an upcoming event, a project, or anything—avoid negative thoughts or thoughts about stressful events.

I believe it was the Los Angeles Dodgers baseball manager Tommy Lasorda who was being interviewed on radio sometime in the 1980s who made a comment regarding stress that I will never forget. Paraphrasing and setting the stage, the World Series games are tied 3–3. It's the seventh and final game of the series and the bottom of the ninth with a score of 6–5, in favor of Los Angeles. There's two outs and a base runner on third. The Los Angeles shortstop hopes his team isn't stressed out with the thought of making a defensive error, so he thinks, *I hope the batter hits this one to me. I will field it, throw him out at first, and we win the series.* Mr. Lasorda used this type of example to explain how a positive thought could overpower a negative and stressful thought.

Who Was Steven Blum?

Steven H. Blum was born on February 21, 1963. Steve was Joanne's oldest of two children and was born with Down syndrome. Joanne and her husband, David, were advised to place Steven in an institution. However, upon visiting such an institution, Joanne and David decided to raise Steven in their wonderful and loving family home environment.

Steve had a natural ability for understanding music and rhythm. Later Steven played the drums for the hometown Bethel, Connecticut, Drum and Fife Corps. The group marched in many parades throughout Connecticut and New York state and also represented the United States in the Irish American festival in Arklow, Ireland.

Steve was an amazing strong avid swimmer. Although I am a certified scuba diver, I never won a race against Steve, pool or open water. Steve was very active with the Special Olympics and earned many medals in swimming competition, most of which are gold medals.

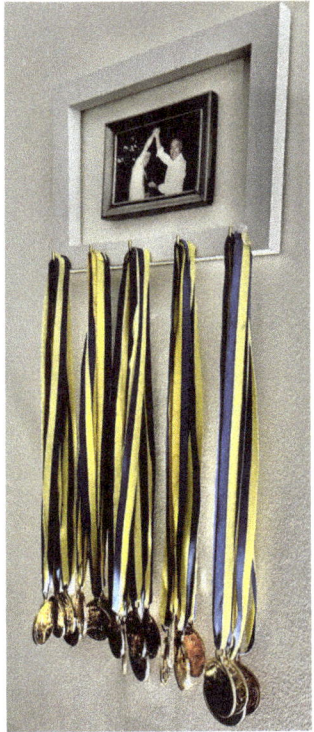

Steven's medals
(Photo by the author)

Steve eventually moved into an Ability Beyond group home (formerly called Datahr and cofounded by Joanne in 1968) in Bethel, Connecticut, and quickly made friends with his new family. Joanne donated the costs for all construction to completely renovate his home to become handicap-accessible, including a deck with handicap ramp and a driveway for a van and ambulance. She also provided an "all-house" standby generator.

Steven's group home was renamed the Blum-Carnevale home
(Photo by the author)

The plaque in the Ability Beyond garden reads: "*In grateful recognition of Ben and Joanne Blum-Carnevale for the opportunities they have made possible for people with disabilities.*" And the stone reads, "*Planted to celebrate a life well lived.*"

Mom and Steven Blum at Blue Jay Orchards in Bethel, Connecticut
(Photo by the author)

After Steven developed Alzheimer's disease, Joanne would drive a four-hour trip every weekend to visit with him. Steve passed away on May 25, 2021. His remains were placed in Buzzards Bay, a favorite swimming area off Cape Cod. In Steve's memory, a bench provided by his family was placed along Peg Noonan Park on Main Street in downtown Falmouth. Steve was a happy, loving person who radiated an abundance of positive energy and thoughts to everyone.

Chapter 3

Thoughts from Nature

Introduction

I believe that most of us have a deep concern, care, and love for all of nature. We learn so much from nature and gather so many positive thoughts. However, we often complain about nature's periods of heavy rain and downpours especially when they last for several days. They affect our plans, our outdoor activities, and we often wish the rain would finally stop; why do we need so much rain? Our roses and tomato plants get adequate water from our garden hoses, but how will all those trees on our planet get watered?

Let's Water the Trees

From its birth to its old age, to its mortality, trees encounter many obstacles. The sun, soil nutrients, and rain strengthen the trees while insects, humans, and storms may weaken or damage them. Depending on the impact of these events, the trees could otherwise have a long, happy, and healthy life. Among the trees, which species will last the longest? I believe the answer depends on the severity of these events. Whenever I travel through the beautiful "green mountain" state of Vermont, I am always amazed at the vast number of trees covering all those beautiful green mountains and for as far as the eyes can see.

All those trees need to be watered periodically, and they need a lot of it in order to penetrate deep down into their rooting systems.

Fire hoses would take much longer than forever. We rely on nature to provide the occasional abundance of rain. After all, trees do need a good drink every now and then, and the only way that can happen is through nature. Nature can quickly and thoroughly accomplish this simple task. How amazing!

Nature is not so concerned about our everyday plans, but instead nature concerns itself with sustaining our lives while maintaining our beautiful environment as well and for all to enjoy. Trees are necessary and so vital for our birds, squirrels, and all wildlife, and we should appreciate nature's remarkable ability to maintain our beautiful trees. Our trees provide food, shelter, shade, pure air, as well as a host of other benefits for us and for our wildlife friends. Our thoughts during heavy rainfalls should be that of the necessity and concerns for our wildlife for we cannot survive without them.

Although tree leaves are designed by nature to guide even the slightest amount of rainfall to their center trunks relative to their tree types and then run down to water their rooting system. Rain is also absorbed by the leaves or needles to nourish the trees. Morning condensation performs the same task as well as provide drinking water for all creatures. Bark, relative to tree types, is designed to also guide the rain to the tree's rooting system.

Electric water pumps used in the fountains on decks, yards, basement sump pumps, and other similar applications are designed to pump water up to specific heights. The higher the need (head), the greater the pump capacity requirement. We have yet to figure out how trees are able to move water from below the ground level up to the tips of every leaf and needle regardless of the height of the tree. Incredible!

The multitude of paths that moisture takes to nourish trees are microscopic. And still no pumps or tools are used or needed! These are my own personal thoughts, which I would like to share with my readers.

After Joanne attended several anesthesia conferences on Cape Cod, Massachusetts, we fell in love with the "Cape" and decided to retire in Falmouth, Cape Cod twenty-three years ago in 1999. After we settled into our new home, among the many fabulous activities on the Cape, one of our favorites was to visit nearby Chapoquoit Beach during the summer as well as during the winter seasons. There are several osprey nests adjacent to Chapoquoit Beach, so during the first spring, we were very excited to observe the little ospreys being fed by their parents.

We watched with our binoculars for longer than we anticipated. And, yes, the nests are still standing as of this writing. The nests were obviously constructed very well and were certainly built to withstand all these years of winter weather (some brutal) as well as rain, sleet, draughts, and exceptional strong winds.

The branches and twigs used for these nests were large and inter-weaved. Why is this so amazing? They were built without the use of nails, ladder, or any other types of conventional construction methods. They were built at the right time and at the right location near water as ospreys exclusively diet on fish. No meetings were ever held, no budgets ever discussed, and no disagreements. Only dedication, determination, and the desire and need to survive and to raise their families. Nature certainly provided ospreys with very effective tools.

Mrs. and Mr. Osprey
(Photo by the author)

We later installed a birdhouse in one of our backyard trees, and soon birds began to occupy the birdhouse. It was so exciting and fun to watch the birds fly back and forth to their "new home." About several weeks after installation, little chicks could be heard. It was so wonderful to watch the parents feed their little ones then quickly fly away to gather more food. Our binoculars are permanently placed by the windows in our sunroom. The little chicks were finally big enough to try out their new wings.

Again, how exciting it was to see them awkwardly flying around with their parents while being taught all the how-tos, and how-not-tos. What touched us most was how the chicks would flutter their little wings while demanding food. We thought, *How could anyone even think about hurting these special and precious creatures, let alone destroy them?* We also thought how wonderful it is that so many actually observe and care about the life of birds.

Many different specious of birds live inside our Leyland trees in our back yard, but it's always sad to eventually see their homes become empty after the little ones grow to adults. But this teaches us hope for we know the new birds will build in the following spring. I got my ladder and carefully observed one of the empty nests. It was still in one piece. What a perfect masterpiece! Again, I thought…no tools and without any outside help.

Several years ago, we went on a very exciting nature walk on Cape Cod, led by the author of a bestseller *The Sibley Guide to Birds*. We observed many birds during our nature walk and learned lots about various species and their habits. We also have several bird feeders in our backyard, and we enjoy watching the cardinals, blue jays, chickadees, American golden finch, and many other species. It is interesting to observe how each have their unique feeding routine and habits.

Outside pets

Among our other outdoor pets are our squirrels and chipmunks. We have many pets now, and it's so exciting to watch them run around and play. The chipmunks fill their cheeks with bird seeds then run into their little holes under our lawn. They are always extra busy preparing for winter storage. How do they know winter is coming? Amazing. Think of the times during extreme poor weather… while we are relaxing by our fireplaces drinking hot coffee in the morning or sipping our favorite drink in the evening, these little warm-blooded creatures that don't hibernate are out there trying to survive. However, some chipmunks will hibernate until next spring.

While Joanne and I enjoy morning coffee on our outside deck, an occasional chipmunk will appear within petting distance. We talk to them, and they seem to know that we are pleased to have them around as our special pets…friends if you will. We're getting close now by actually hand-feeding them…how exciting it is to know they trust us. I have often commented there is nothing more gratifying than to have the friendship and trust of a wild animal. They are our little friends, and we are trying to take care and protect them.

Many years ago, I was sitting in my hotel room on the twenty-third floor in St. Louis watching TV while taking a break from the annual steel guitar convention when I noticed a flock of Canada geese out my window flying in perfect V formation across the Mississippi River and heading east toward Illinois. I then watched several more flocks repeatedly flying the same route. They were also flying at the same angle while crossing the Mississippi. Many of us cannot explain how geese (as well as other bird species) know which bearings to take or how it's even possible. There have also been many theories, and the one that I tend to favor is their inherent magnetic field…after all, we use the compass or GPS to find our way.

Joanne and I were driving into our neighborhood one afternoon when we suddenly discovered a baby robin on the road struggling to fly. We stopped the car, picked the bird up, and brought it home. Being a nurse anesthetist, I knew Joanne would know the right thing to do. She immediately decided to call the Cape Cod Wildlife for advice.

Little "Robbie"
(Photo by the author)

We were advised to place the little bird in the exact location where we found it, and that its mother would find and take care of it. We did just that. It was very difficult to leave that little bird alone, but we were confident that its mother would hear her baby and take care of it. That's what mothers do. This experience created a flow of many positive thoughts.

Goose Story

Reading the goose Story gives us a much better understanding and appreciation for these incredible birds. I will never understand why some ignore or even destroy these precious creatures. Their life can be a lesson in teaching us about life, especially right from wrong.

I have included the following for the those that haven't read the goose story:

> *When you see geese flying along in V formation you might consider what science has discovered as to why they fly that way. As each bird flaps its wings, it creates an updraft for the bird immediately following. By flying in V formation, the whole flock adds at least 71 percent greater flying range than if each bird flew separately on its own. People who share a common direction and the sense of community can get where they are going more quickly and easily because they are traveling on the thrust of one another.*
>
> *When a goose falls out of formation, it suddenly feels the drag and resistance of trying to do it alone and quickly gets back into formation to take advantage of the lifting power of the bird in front. If we have as much sense as a goose, we will stay in formation with those people who are headed the same way we are.*
>
> *When the head of the geese gets tired, it rotates back in the wing and another goose flies at the point position. It is sensible to take turns doing demanding jobs, whether with people or with geese flying south. Geese honk from behind one another to encourage those up front to keep up their speed.*
>
> *What messages do we give when we honk from behind? Finally, when a goose gets sick or is wounded by gunshot and falls out of formation, two other geese fall out with that goose and follow it down to lend help and protection. They stay with the fallen goose until it is able to fly or until it dies and only then do they launch out on their own, or with another formation, to catch up with their group. If we have the sense of a goose, we will stand by each other like that.*
>
> (Author unknown)

Canada geese
(Photo by the author)

Story of the Butterfly

If you haven't read the story of the butterfly, you will find it to be very inspiring:

Monarch butterfly cocoon
(Photo courtesy of the US Department of Agriculture)

A man found a cocoon of a butterfly. One day, a small opening appeared. He watched the butterfly for several hours as it struggled to force its body through that little hole. Then it seemed to stop making any progress.

It appeared as if it had gotten as far as it could, and it would go no further. So the man decided to help the butterfly. He took a pair of scissors and snipped off the remaining bit of the cocoon. The butterfly then emerged easily. But it had a swollen body and small, shriveled wings.

The man expected that, at any moment, the wings would enlarge and expand to be able to support the body, which would contract in time. Neither happened. The butterfly spent the rest of his life crawling around with a swollen body and shriveled wings. It was never able to fly. What the man in his kindness and haste did not understand was that the struggle required the butterfly to get through the tiny opening was God's way of forcing the fluid from the body of the butterfly to its wings so that it would be ready for flight once it achieved its freedom from the cocoon.

Sometimes struggles are exactly what we need in our life. If God allows us to go through our life without any obstacles, it will cripple us. We would not be as strong as we could have been; we could never fly. (Author unknown)

Monarch butterfly
(Photo courtesy of US Department of Agriculture)

I asked God for strength, and He gave me difficulties to make me strong.
I asked God for wisdom, and He gave me a problem to solve.
I asked God for prosperity, and He gave me a brain and brawn to work.
I asked God for courage, and He gave me danger to overcome.
I asked God for love, and He gave me troubled people to help.
I asked God for favors, and He gave me opportunities.
I received nothing I wanted, but I received everything I needed.
(Author unknown)

I have received so much inspiration from reading quotes about nature that I thought I would share a few with my readers.

"Look deep into nature, and then you will understand everything better" (Albert Einstein).

"My scientific work is motivated by an irresistible longing to understand the secrets of nature and not by other feelings" (Albert Einstein).

Are we intelligent, or are we smart?

There's a big difference. Being intelligent is having the ability to acquire knowledge, whereas being smart is the ability to apply knowledge in a practical manner. I believe that we all possess both but either at a high level or at a lower level. Nevertheless, we inherently possess both. In simple terms, we have the ability to acquire knowledge as a child then physically apply it. Later in life, we may acquire a vast amount of knowledge from major universities, for example, but are we smart enough to apply our knowledge in a practical sense?

Listening to the silence

While stationed in Michigan, I would take several furloughs to my home in Massachusetts several times a year including Christmas. I left the air force base on December 22, 1953, early one evening around 6:00 or 7:00 PM so that I could travel through Canada during the night and reach the New York–Massachusetts line by early morning. One of my exceptional nature experiences was while driving through the Berkshire Mountains in western Massachusetts on the Mohawk Trail (Rt. 2) in my yellow and brown 1951 Nash Rambler. The Massachusetts Turnpike did not exist in the early 1950s, so I would connect from the New York State Thruway near the Albany area onto the Mohawk Trail, which was a simple two-lane road with no side shoulders. Trees were beautifully situated along each side of the road. I continued driving the full length of the Mohawk Trail to my home in the western suburb of Boston.

I was on the summit of a mountain, taking in all of nature's beauty. It was a clear and bright sunny morning, and all the tree branches on the Mohawk Trail were covered with glittering ice. I just had to stop and get out of my car. I stood along the side of the road, looked all around, and listened to the silence. I had never experienced such beauty. There were no stores, no traffic, or were there any homes, only an occasional farm and barns. I experienced the most peaceful and awesome relationship with nature. My mind was saturated with positive thoughts.

Politics?

Some of my readers may remember the political atmosphere which I first experienced in the mid to late 1940s. The candidate you voted for was sacred. A secret never discussed. It was simply no one's business. In fact, it was unethical. Citizens would vote at their designated precincts, and that was it. No one would ever ask, and you would never tell. There was no reason to do so. Americans respected Americans. Revealing such secrets as we do today would only open the door to arguments or attempts to convince otherwise.

Secrecy prevents such situations. You voted for whoever you thought was the best candidate for your interests and for your country. It was your choice.

There were no conservative or liberal hosts on radio or TV programs to fabricate stories or situations to desperately convince you otherwise. In fact, there were no radios or TVs during that time. How wonderful…how reassuring…how American. Voting for your candidate for whatever reasons, inserts positive thoughts, and in my opinion, should never be challenged. Today's political agendas have changed everything from causing doubts to loosing friendships.

Can we fly?

Did you ever wish that you could fly like a bird? I believe most of us get that feeling now and then. Well, we can come pretty close to it. The air is very thin, so we certainly can't fly through air, but water is about 25 percent more dense than air. We can go underwater in a pool or an ocean and snorkel or scuba dive. We can "fly" up, down, and visit all around. When swimming underwater, I love imagining that I'm really flying. It takes on a whole new perspective than just simply swimming.

Chapter 4

Thoughts from Flowers and Plants

Introduction

Everyone loves flowers and plants! Safe to say, nearly everyone has plants in their home and in their gardens. I marvel at the thought of looking at a beautiful flower, such as a rose for example, and while taking in all the beauty of its shape, color, size, aroma, and softness, I realize that its viewing is all for free. We are looking at one of nature's most beautiful wonders without invoking any obligations on our part. None at all!

It's amazing beauty along with its dangerous thorns provides nature's lesson to us. *"Take the bad with the good."* But what amazes me is that all this beauty was created by one not-so-beautiful tiny seed placed in dirty soil! Another lesson from nature, *"It matters not what we were, it matters what we are and what we will become."*

Can plants remember? It isn't known if all plants have the ability to remember, but in a study, sixty potted plants known to fold their leaves when touched or threatened were individually dropped from several inches during sixty consecutive times. All plants curled their leaves during the first few times they were dropped but then remained open during the remainder of the experiment once they realized they were in no real danger.

During a second experiment, the pots were placed in a machine and shaken. Realizing this was a new threat, all plants folder their leave until they again realized they were in no real danger at which time their leaves remained open during the remainder of the experiment.

Azaleas

Azaleas grow well in acidic soils from 4.5 to 6.0 pH and good drainage. Azaleas do not favor clay soil. They like 50 percent sun and shade. They will not bloom in dense shade, and they will burn in full sun. Plant azaleas in the spring or in the fall and prune in the spring after blooming.

Box Elder

Box elder plants fool many of us into thinking they are poison ivy! Notice there are two sets of three leaves on a common stem. That's a definite clue for identifying that they are not poison ivy or any other type of poison plant. But it's amazing how box elder plants can look so much like poison ivy but with just enough differences to make identification possible. Whenever I'm in doubt I look for another identifier before I'm totally convinced, such as the length of the stem of the middle leaf. If the stem is longer than the stems on the outer two leaves, then I have found the perfect clue!

Box elder plant

Boxwood

The American boxwood plant is a wide spreading shrub or a small tree with very dense evergreen foliage. Boxwoods may reach twenty feet but are typically five to ten feet tall. The leaves are dark green on the upper side and yellow green on the underside. Leaves are about 1 1/2 inches long, oval in shape, and are tolerant of cold weather. Boxwoods are commonly used in landscaping residential homes, foundation, corner areas, privacy, gardens, and public grounds. These plants are also used in many historical gardens and modern contemporary homes.

Boxwood provides many other landscape uses such as

- background for other plants;
- pattern or framework in formal gardens;
- outlining parking areas, flower borders, and walkways; and
- planter boxes or large plant containers.

Boxwood plant
(Photo by the author)

They have a wide range in size and growth. Low or tall, as well as fast or slow growers, are available. There are also interesting variations available in size of foliage as well as various texture characteristics.

Planting boxwoods

Plant in well-drained soils and not near downspouts or in any area that remains wet. Boxwoods grow best in semi shade. A soil sample should be taken before planting. The planting hole should be twice as wide and as deep as the root ball. Use a good quality topsoil around the root ball to encourage root growth. Deep planting may cause loss of plant strength and eventual death. After planting, water thoroughly. Light watering may encourage a buildup of salts which can damage their root system.

Mulching boxwoods

Boxwoods grow poorly in hot, dry soils. Add two to three inches of mulch, such as bark mulch or wood chips, over the soil surface. Do not place black plastic under the mulch, and do not use pine needles as mulch since they may be detrimental to boxwoods. Check annually and add more mulch as the depth decreases due to decomposition. Mulching keeps the plant root system cool, retains moisture by slowing down evaporation from the soil, and reduces weed problems.

Fertilizing boxwoods

Test the soil in the fall prior to fertilizing. Near coastal areas, fertilize twice during the growing season. The first application should be made in early spring before plant shoot growth starts. The second application should be made during midsummer. Avoid a late-summer application as it can force tender growth that may be subject to frost damage. Keep fertilizers off the plant leaves and never closer than several inches from the stem. Rinse plant foliage after fertilizing then water thoroughly.

Pruning boxwoods

Remove older inner branches to encourage new branch development then prune the plant to increase density or to maintain a desired size or shape. However, use caution as frequent removal of inner branches may create exceptional dense foliage, causing increased inner shade, which results in foliage drop.

Watering boxwood plants

Newly planted boxwoods must be watered to keep the roots from drying out. Instead of frequent and light watering, let the water hose run slowly so the root system can soak completely. Lack of sufficient moisture in the spring and summer months may cause late growth in the fall due to heavy rains resulting in damage during freezing weather.

Cultivating boxwood plants

Cultivating deeply around boxwoods could injure their shallow roots. Avoid doing this. Damaged portion of the plant showing injury are typically caused by severed roots.

Prevent winter damage

Check to see that the center of the plant is free of dead leaves and other debris. Water during dry periods throughout the year. If fertilizer is needed, apply before July, and do necessary pruning during the spring to develop strong stems. Provide wind protection by using snow fences or cover with burlap. Do not allow the burlap to touch the foliage. Mulch protects the plant by preventing rapid temperature change on the soil surface, deep penetration of frost, and excessive loss of surface water. Remove snow from boxwoods during or after a snowstorm or as soon as practical by brushing the plant with a broom. The weight of heavy snow may cause the stems to break.

However, do not attempt to remove snow if branches are frozen. Avoid planting boxwoods under the eaves in the path of possible snow avalanches. Large American boxwoods may be protected against snow damage by tying the outer branches in such a way to prevent breakage from excess weight of snow or ice.

Bulbs

Bulbs may be planted any time that the ground is not frozen. Planting earlier in the year is best. Planting deeper will assure that the bulbs will maintain a more constant temperature, whereas shallower is subject to damage from temperature fluctuations.

Compost

Pine needles make good winter compost around the base of some plants. Oak leaves are also excellent. Mix with grass clippings to speed composting. Never use whole leaves as they produce terrible mulch.

Corn

The male part of the corn sprouts out from the top where the pollen is created. Corn silk (as many as six hundred strands) is the key part of the female reproductive system and essential for corn pollination. These silks are where grains of pollen land. The pollen then travels down the silk strands to the unfertilized ear inside the husk. Another function of the silk along with the husk is to protect and help the corn kernels hold their moisture and retain their sweetness.

Native Americans, as well as other countries such as China and Turkey, have been using corn silk as herbal medical remedies for centuries. Studies show that corn silk contains carbohydrates, fiber, calcium, iron, sodium, potassium, zinc, chloride, and protein. Although corn silk may be eaten or used to make tasty tea or dried and blended for toppings, advise from your medical professional is always first recommended.

Cut Flowers

To keep cut flowers fresh, start with the freshest flowers available. If you are cutting flowers from your garden, cut them in the morning after the dew has dried. If you plan on purchasing the flowers, then buy as soon as they become available.

Choose flowers with buds and shiny leaves and get the flowers into water as soon as possible. Use a vase that won't crowd the flowers. Before trimming stems, remove any foliage that will be below the waterline. Submerged foliage degrades quickly and encourages the growth of bacteria, which gums up the flowers' stems and reduces their ability to take up water.

Place the stems under running water and cut off about one inch from each stem at a forty-five-degree angle. Use a sharp knife or pruners rather than household scissors, which can crush the stems. Immediately place the freshly cut flowers into the vase. Place your arrangement away from direct sunlight. Trim off one-fourth inch of the stems every other day in the same manner and change the water in the vase.

Cuttings

Cut stems just below a bud and below where a leaf attaches to its stem (node). Roots will develop easier when cut from this location. Do not cut well below the node as rot will likely occur. Remove the flowers and lower leaves from the cutting, otherwise the flower may attempt to seed, thus rob the cutting of needed food. Fill a container with potting mix, insert the cuttings about one inch into the mix, then soak with water to provide a moist contact between the mix and the cuttings.

Place the container inside a plastic bag to build humidity and moisture. Insert bamboo stakes or pencils into the mix with eraser end up to prevent the bag from sagging. Do not allow the bag to make contact with the cuttings, otherwise mold may occur. Close the bag with twist ties and check weekly to assure the mix is moist. Water slightly when there is no evidence of condensation of moisture in the plastic bag. After several weeks when the roots have established, place the cuttings in separate pots and in the shade until the new plants become adjusted to their new environment.

Daisies

If you plant daisies in the fall, they will bloom from July through September. Typical height is about eighteen inches. However, trim them to the desired height in the spring. Daisies love full sunlight. Daisies come in many colors, except blue. Their leaves are edible and a great source of vitamin C. Daisies have medicine properties and known to soothe coughs, slow bleeding, and relieve indigestion. Daisies are actually two flowers blended together in harmony, and so they represent the meaning of true love. Daises are special for any romantic occasion. The sunflower is daisy's giant cousin.

Dirt

What is dirt? Dirt is made up of a mixture of dead organic matter and does not contain the minerals and nutrients found in soil. Dirt does not have a set structure, which explains why dirt doesn't compact when moisture is added. Since dirt is dead and lacks nutrients, it can't support or nurture plant life. You can't plant a successful and thriving garden using dirt.

Edelweiss Flower

The edelweiss flower is the symbol of Switzerland and grows high up in the mountains. This is a perennial plant about six inches tall. In Switzerland, the edelweiss plant is protected by law. The Swiss edelweiss flower signifies noble purity and is the insignia of the Austrian, Polish, Romanian, and German alpine troops. The insignia is also worn by the United States Army First Battalion Tenth Special Forces group, airborne soldiers.

Edelweiss Flower
Author: Daniel Schwen. This photo is subject
to a Creative Commons License
https://creativecommons.org/licenses/by-sa/4.0/
deed.en#ref-appropriate-credit.
No changes were made to this photo.

Fertilize

Shrubs, trees, and perennials

Use organic fertilizers in late fall or in winter. Use chemical fertilizers in late spring. Always use compost manure and not fresh manure because compost manure eliminates the odor typical with fresh manure and has less moisture, making it lighter and easier to handle. Compost manure may also kill weed and seeds. Proper fertilizing of grass will produce a light shade of bright green. If a lawn is a very deep dark green, this is a sign that the lawn was heavily fertilized with an excessive amount of nitrogen.

Grass

The ideal pH for lawn soil should be acidic at 5.5. If the pH is too high, grass cannot absorb nutrients properly. Lime is typically spread to raise the pH while sulfur is spread to lower the pH.

Heather

The ideal soil pH for heather plants should be about 4.5 to 5.5 acid soil. If the soil is too alkaline, add peat moss to lower the pH. Heather seldom needs water, but good drainage is recommended. Prune in the spring. Heather plants need at least a half day of sun or a minimum of six hours of sun a day. Full sun is better as the foliage colors intensify when fully exposed. Too much shade makes these plants leggy and affects the brilliance of their color.

Hydrangeas

Do not remove dead-looking stocks; instead, wait until late spring then remove only the stocks without buds. Prune the remaining stalks down to the new growth.

Drying hydrangea flowers

Near the end of the blooming season, you may notice that the larger flowers have smaller flowers on their tops. Just before the smaller flowers open, cut their stems about fifteen inches from the base of the flower and remove all leaves from the stems. Place the cut flowers into a vase filled with water and away from direct sun. After the water has completely evaporated, the hydrangeas should be dry and ready to spray paint if you want to change color or use them for craft making.

Hydrangea pH

Typically, acidic soil with a pH lower than 6.0 yields blue or lavender/blue hydrangea blooms. Alkaline soil with a pH above 7.0 yields pink and red blooms. With a pH between 6 and 7, the blooms turn purple or bluish/pink.

Leyland Cypress

Leyland cypress trees are fast-growing and popular as a landscape tree for privacy and hedges. They are relatively free from serious disease problems. However, there are a few common diseases that we need to be concerned about, such as canker fungus and needle blight.

Fungus disease

This disease is caused by cold weather or from drought conditions, which may occur during early spring. This disease usually enters through cracks and wounds in the branches and bark. Cankers leak a brown, thick, and sticky resin substance. Infected branches should be pruned and destroyed. Pruning during dry periods will minimize spreading the disease. In addition to periodic pruning, watering will help Leyland to become resilient to such infections.

Needle blight

Needle blight

Needle blight is browning of the needles. This disease spreads until only the needles at the tips of the upper branches remain green. Damage results from feeding by caterpillars, which causes loss of needles. Heavy infestations can kill the tree altogether. This disease is best controlled by spraying with fungicides containing copper.

Juniper scale

Juniper scale infection cause Leyland to appear off-color. Infected branches may have little growth, and the needles may turn yellow or brown. Shiny, sticky material is often seen on needles of Leyland infected with juniper scale.

Lavender

Lavender (*lavare*) means "to wash." The lavender herb is a popular ingredient we use to bathe, shampoo, for facial cleansers, hand soap, as well as many medicinal uses, such as to soothe burns, help with sleep, reduce stress, treat aching muscles and joints, and a remedy for headaches and indigestion. During the sixteenth century black plague, lavender oil was used to remove the smell of the dead. Lavender represents purity, serenity, and devotion and is available in white, yellow, or pink. Lavender is a popular choice for flower arrangements and wedding bouquets.

Lichen

I love lichen. I love to look really closely and observe how they attach themselves to tree branches and rocks, and I love to feel their rubbery or firm texture and love their many vivid colors. Among their many functions, lichen breaks down boulders and rocks to make new soil, and they make existing soil richer with nutrients. Lichen also provides a source of food for deer and other similar wildlife animals. The presence of lichen lets us know that the quality of the air is pure.

However, lichens do not harm trees and shrubs because they do not enter the inner bark where food is transported and, therefore, cannot rob the trees of nourishment or do they cause disease. Lichen on trees indicate the air nearby is relatively pure as lichens will not grow in a polluted atmosphere. Damaged plants simply give lichens access to the sun they need for growth.

Lichen is a complex organism formed by alga and fungus. Lichens appears in the form of small patchy crusty outgrowths in colors of green, brown, orange, as well as other colors, and are found on rocks, tree trunks, and moist soil. There are about twenty-five thousand species of lichen living only on air, light, and minerals.

Lichen forming and living on a boulder
(Photo by the author)

Lichen produce acids that split up rocks, which helps the lichen to get a better grip on its base and also aids in the erosion process of turning rocks into soil. In some countries, lichen is edible.

Lichen also provides building materials and shelters for many wildlife animals, such as deer, elk, birds, and insects. However, some lichens are poisonous. The wolf lichen, for example, was used by American Indians for poisonous arrowheads. Ground lichen is another poisonous lichen, which caused tissue decay and eventual death when it was consumed in Wyoming in 2004 by hundreds of visiting elks from Colorado. The native Wyoming elk were not affected as they became immune to this toxic lichen. Ground lichen has been known to also poison cattle. Japan uses lichens in paint for its anti-mildew properties. Some lichens are used in developing antibiotic drugs as well as other products, such as deodorant and toothpaste. Egyptians used lichen to pack bodies during the embalming process. It is highly absorbent as well as possessing aromatic qualities.

Certain species of lichen, such as oak moss, has been commercial used for fragrance in the perfume industry. Lichen is often used for model train landscaping, floral arrangements, and craft projects.

Mayflower Plant

The mayflower is the state flower for Massachusetts because it was the first flower found by the Pilgrims. The mayflower is also the first flower to bloom in the spring in Massachusetts.

The Mayflower Plant
(Photo courtesy of the US Department of Agriculture)

Palm Trees

Can we tell the age of a palm tree? No, we can't because they don't develop rings, and they cannot be carbon dated. After the leaves fall off, palm trees regrow new leaves. In addition to coconuts, many palm trees also provide fruit, dates, nuts, and oil.

Palm wine is a common wine made in some areas of Africa and Asia and can be made from date palms, coconut palms, and the Chilean wine palm!

The needle palm is so hardy it can even be grown in Alaska. The coco de mer palm tree can grow to heights exceeding one hundred feet with leaves over thirty feet long. This palm takes up to fifty years to reach maturity. The seeds alone can weigh over sixty pounds and grow up to twenty inches in diameter!

Perennials

After the first hard frost, cut away the old stock and foliage to about three inches above the ground. To divide perennial plants, do so from early fall to mid-October or during early spring.

pH

The term pH stands for "potential hydrogen" or "power of hydrogen" (the "p" is lowercased while the "H" is uppercased). The pH scale is 0 to 14 and used to tell the amount of hydrogen a substance, such as water or soil, contains and how active the hydrogen ions are, with 0 being the highest acidity and no alkaline, 7 being natural, and 14 being the highest alkaline and no acidity. The pH scale is logarithmic, meaning that for every change of 1 on the scale reflects 10 times change. For example, 3 on the scale is 10 times stronger than 2 on the scale, and conversely, 2 is 10 times weaker than 3 on the scale. Readings that are under pH 7.0 means higher concentrations of hydrogen, thus resulting in a substance with more acid and less alkaline contents. Whereby, readings over pH 7.0 means a lower concentration of hydrogen, thus resulting in a substance with more alkaline, less acid contents.

To decrease the pH of soil and cause it to be more acidic, add components such as sulfur (slow reacting) or aluminum sulfate (fast reacting). To increase the pH of soil and cause it to be more alkaline, add components containing calcium or magnesium, such as lime, baking soda, oyster shells, wood ashes, or eggshells.

pH recommended

Shrubs	pH
Azale	4.5 to 6.0
Barberry	6.0 to 7.0
Boxwood	5.6 to 7.0
Camellia	5.5 to 5.5
Euonymus	6.0 to 8.0
Flowering Almond	7.0 to 8.5
Gardenia	5.0 to 6.0
Hibiscus	6.1 to 6.5
Huckleberry	4.5 to 5.5
Hydrangea (blue)	<6.0
Hydrangea (purple)	6.0 to 7.0
Hydrangea (pink)	>7.0
Lilac	6.5 to 7.0
Rhododendron	5.0 to 5.5
Tea Roses	6.5 to 7.0

Trees	pH
Apple	6.5 to 7.0
Cherry	6.0 to 6.5
Crab Apple	5.0 to 6.5
Dogwood	5.5 to 6.0
Elm	6.0 to 7.5
Holly	5.0 to 6.0
Magnolia	5.5 to 6.5
Maple	5.0 to 7.0
Pear	6.0 to 6.5
Pin Oak	5.0 to 7.0
Pine	4.5 to 6.0

Red Oak	5.0 to 7.0
Scarlet Oak	6.0 to 7.0
Weeping Willow	5.0 to 6.0

Flowers	**pH**
Amaryllis	6.0 to 6.5
Baby's Breath	7.0 to 7.5
Begonia	5.5 to 6.5
Carnation	6.5 to 7.0
Chrysanthemum	6.5 to 7.0
Daffodil	6.0 to 7.0
Dahlia	6.5 to 7.0
Day Lily	6.3 to 6.8
Easter Lily	6.5 to 7.0
Geranium	5.8 to 6.2
Gladiolus	6.0 to 6.5
Hollyhock	6.0 to 8.0
Iris	6.8
Marigold	6.0 to 7.0
Narcissus	6.0 to 7.0
Pansy	5.4 to 5.8
Periwinkle	6.5 to 7.5
Petunia	6.0 to 7.0
Phlox	5.0 to 6.0
Poppy	6.5 to 7.0
Snapdragon	6.2 to 7.0
Sweet Pea	7.0 to 8.0
Sweet William	6.5 to 7.5
Touch-Me-Not	6.0 to 7.0
Tulip	6.0 to 7.0
Zinnia	5.5 to 7.5

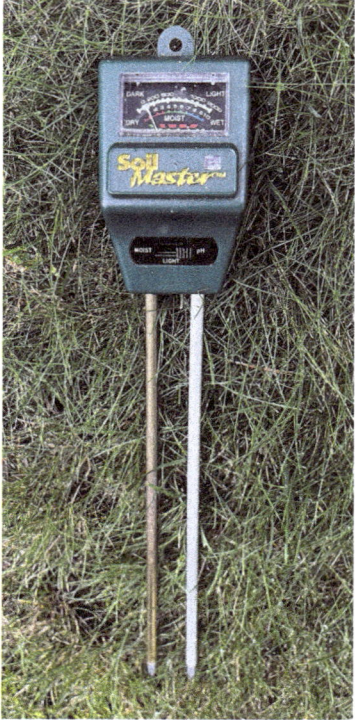

pH meter
(Photo by the author)

Use a pH meter to check the pH of your soil. Be sure the soil is damp and that the two rods are free of soil and moisture before inserting into the soil.

Phlox

How can we remove unsightly grass growing inside phlox flowers? Dig up the phlox plants and remove all the grass. Be sure to get a big root ball when you dig them up. Place down newspapers and cardboard, cut holes in the newspapers, and replant the phlox. Then spread mulch about two to three inches deep. Water every day until the phlox roots become established. It should then be a simple matter to remove any grass within the flowers.

Pitch Pines

Cape Cod native pitch pines prefer shallow, sandy soil and need full sun to grow. Upper section grows toward the sun while the lower section branches periodically die, leaving a long and naked trunk. Pitch pines have three needle clusters. The pitch pine tree derives its name from the high resin content in its wood. American Indians used pitch pine trees not only for canoes but also for medicines to treat rheumatism, burns, cuts, boils, and as a laxative.

Pitch pine's three-needle cluster
(Photo by the author)

Prune or trim pitch pines only in late fall otherwise. Beetles may be attracted to the sap at the cuts and will infect the tree as well as other surrounding trees. The cut areas will naturally heal themselves. The sap from pitch pines is clear but turns black when exposed. Colonists used this tar for a lubricant on wagon wheel axles.

Poison Ivy, Poison Oak, and Poison Sumac

Poisonous plants are not the only plants with leaves in clusters of three. However, "leaves of three, leave them be" is a good rule of thumb to avoiding them. Poison ivy, poison oak, and poison sumac are in the same family and contain the same skin irritant called "urushiol" (you-roo-she-ol) oil. After contacting any one of these poison plants, the symptoms of the rash that may develop can worsen within a few days. It's easy to advise "not to scratch" the affected areas, but doing so can cause the situation to worsen and infection to set in.

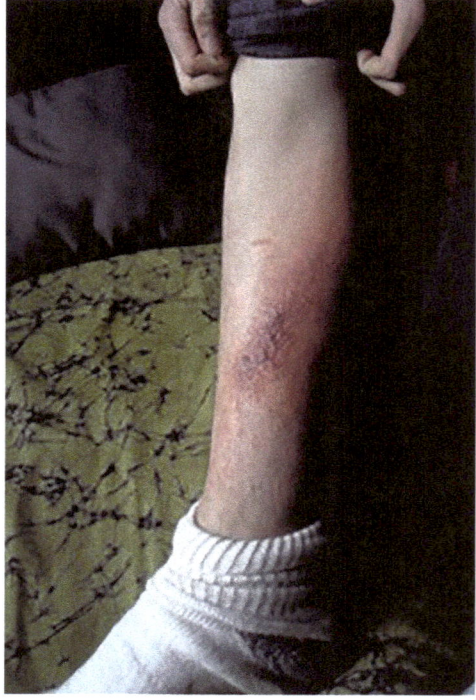

Typical rash from poisonous plants

What causes the rash?

The urushiol oil is in the roots, stems, and the leaves whether the plant is alive, dried up, or dead. Tearing out vines can be dangerous. Doing so could spray large amounts of urushiol. This oil causes skin reactions in the form of a rash after making contact. We can get a poison rash even during the winter. Urushiol oils from poisonous plants can be transferred from animal, garden tools, and clothing to your skin upon contact. Never burn poison plants since the airborne vapors can cause inflammation of the airway if inhaled. Some people appear to be immune to poison plants; however, do not assume you can't get it even though you've never had it before. People change with age. It takes about forty-eight hours to manifest, so as soon as you realize that you came in contact with it, quickly wash the area with mild water and soap.

What's it like to get it?

At first you get a slight itchy spot, which becomes worse. The rash can get huge and ugly and can be one of the itchiest experiences. The rash can last anywhere from one to three weeks depending on its severity. You may consider using jewelweed to help the rash. Squeeze the jewelweed and apply its liquid to the areas of the rash or check with your doctor to see if early treatment can prevent the rash from becoming worse.

Pets and the poison rash

Animals cannot get a rash from poison plants. Deer, goats, and other similar grazing animals eat poisonous plant leaves while wild birds eat their seeds. However, many people do get a rash from the urushiol oil on the coat of animals or their pets. Wash your pet then wash yourself as well.

Is it contagious?

Once you have the rash, the oil has already been absorbed, and you probably can't spread it to others or elsewhere on yourself. If you get large blisters filled with liquid, it is mostly water and will not spread the rash even should they break although many feel that the fluid spreads and causes further outbreaks.

Poisonous plant symptoms

Symptoms of poisonous plant rash develop within seven days after exposure to the poison plant depending on how much urushiol was present and the thickness of the skin. A poison rash has the following features:

- Itching
- Painful blisters that are filled with fluid
- Red blotches that may appear in streaks
- Swelling

Avoiding poisonous plants

Wear long pants, a long-sleeve shirt, shoes, and long socks. Wear gloves that completely cover your shirt sleeves. Do not touch any of your exposed skin areas. Stay in the middle of walking trails and learn to recognize all three poisonous plants.

Treatments

Wash everything with water and soap after any exposure to help remove the urushiol oil to minimize your chances of developing a rash.

Home remedies for poison rash

Some over-the-counter (OTC) remedies may help relieve the itching and shorten the overall time span. Topical steroid creams and gels may lessen inflammation and help the poison rash to heal faster. Also consider Calamine Lotion, Aveeno Anti-Itch Cream, Cortisone, or apply a wet or cold compresses to the itchy areas several times a day. When the rash becomes impossible to resist scratching, here's a remedy that I discovered years ago that works very well for me. It not only makes my poison rash "feel good," but it actually cures the rash in a much faster time.

When rashes appear and become extremely itchy beyond tolerant, I run hot water full blast with no mixture of cold water. I place my hands under the hot water while manipulating a bar of soap at amazing speeds. Don't worry, you'll be able to handle the hot water, assuming the hot water thermostat is typically set for the normal 120°F, which I believe is recommended for everyday use and for sterile dishwasher use. If the water seems too hot, adjust the valves until the hot becomes tolerable. My hot water tank is set to provide 110°F, which is perfect for my needs.

It will burn a bit, but it will feel really good! After about thirty seconds, some of the blisters may open, but the soap, along with the rubbing action and the constant water flow will remove and send the detrimental oils down the drain. I continue doing this until it "feels good," then I turn off the water and pat dry. The itching is gone, and the hands look red but feel much better. After a few minutes, I'm back or close to normal again. In other areas of my body, I scrub the rash(es) using hot water and a washcloth while showering.

Medical attention for poison rash

Your doctor can prescribe antibiotics or other types of medication to help speed up the healing process or for more serious symptoms, such as trouble swallowing, shortness of breath, swelling, especially of the face, and fever.

Poison Ivy Plants

There are basically two types of poison ivy plants, the climbing vine and the non-climbing vine. The climbing type is considered the eastern poison ivy and is native to New England. The center leaflet has a slightly longer stem than the other two leaflets as noted reddish center in the photo below. The edges of the leaves may be smooth or serrated. The main stems are reddish in color.

Both types have three leaves on common thornless stems. The young poison ivy may display reddish, droopy leaves while mature leaves are smooth and turn red and yellow in the fall. Then small yellow flowers bloom close to the vine of the plant in the spring. In the summer, the blossoms change to colored berries. The plant is invasive and difficult to kill because the stems can root where they make contact with the ground and potentially become new plants.

New England eastern climbing poison ivy plant
(Photo by the author)

Poison ivy locations

We are all aware that poison ivy plants of either type can be found in forests, wetlands, beaches, walking trails, along streams, as well as in residential yards. They thrive in partial shade but not so much in completely shaded areas or sunny areas. Both types grow in all states except Alaska, Hawaii, Washington, and in the deserts. Both types look similar, give a similar rash, and can be found together in the same locations.

Poison Oak Plants

Poison oak is a woody shrub generally identified by its three oily leaves on common stems, with leaf-rounded edges somewhat similar to oak tree leaves but fuzzy on the underside. The leaves can be green, yellow, or red, and they fall off each year. The center leaf stem is longer than the other two leaflets.

Poison oak plant
(Photo courtesy of the US Department of Agriculture)

Poison Sumac Plants

Poison Sumacs are found in eastern United States and in Canada. When it comes to poison sumac, the three-leaf rule doesn't apply. These plants can have seven to thirteen smooth-edged leaflets. The leaflet stems are always red. When burned, inhaling the smoke may cause diarrhea and internal irritations. The poison sumac is a woody shrub or small tree that can grow up to about twenty feet tall. Yellow/green flowers are present during June and July. Small white or gray berries are visible in September as opposed to nonpoisonous sumacs, which have red berries. Poison sumac have shorter leaves, fewer leaflets, and smooth-edged oval leaflets arranged in pairs along its stem with one leaflet on the end of its branch as opposed to the leaf arrangement in nonpoisonous sumacs. The leaves are bright orange in the spring, dark green in the summer, and red orange during the fall.

They exclusively grow in extreme wet or flooded areas, such as watery swampy wetlands, whereby nonpoisonous sumacs are found in dry soil.

Poison sumac plant
(Photo courtesy of the US Department of Agriculture)

Poison sumacs include these features:

- No hair on stems
- Leaflet about two to four inches long
- Leaflets are oval to oblong in shape
- Leaflets tapering to a sharp point
- Leaflets undersides are hairless

Pollen

What is the purpose of pollen?

The main purpose of pollen is to transfer male reproductive sperms to female reproductive ovules, thus allowing sexual reproduction. The pollen receptive part of the flower is often sticky or textured so the pollen can stick. Once attached, the pollen grain grows a tube eventually into the ovule. This tube allows fertilization of the ovule, thus creating a seed. Pollen can be transferred by many methods, such as wind, gravity, and insects. However, most trees, such as the beach, chestnut, maple, oak, and pine, distribute their pollen by means of the wind.

1. Pollen never deteriorates. It is one of the few natural secreted substances that last indefinitely.
2. Pollen is found mainly in hardwood trees.
3. Rain cleans air of pollen.
4. Pollen is highest in mornings. Do outside work in the afternoons.
5. Keep the car and home windows closed during pollen season.

Pruning

"If brown, cut it down but leave several inches above the ground." Pinch or cut off the brown branch tips just above green leaves. Do this to all plants including tomato plants before the flower buds start. Pinching will cause the bush or plant to become more dense and produce more flowers or fruits.

Pumpkins

Male flowers on pumpkins contains pollen while female flowers produce the pumpkin fruit. Bees transfer pollen from the male flowers to the female flowers to produce more pumpkins.

Rhododendron

Prune very soon after flowing stops, otherwise buds will begin to form and pruning is not advisable until flowering ends during the next year.

Roses

Rose plants are pollution tolerant, and that's why they are popular in the cities. Flowers or buds will fall off quickly if the soil is dry.

This plant needs lots of moisture and grow best with three inches of quality mulch around its base.

Soak the roots in water just before planting. Transplant roses in early spring. Prune for ease while transplanting. Prune early in the spring to allow sealing the cut, otherwise winter could freeze the stems.

Rose of Sharon

Rose of Sharon plants may look dead but wait until the end of May for signs of life. These plants bloom from midsummer until fall.

Pruning rose of Sharon

If you don't prune, flowers will be small but many. However, if you do prune, flowers will be large but few. To control height, prune anytime.

Sedum Autumn Fire

What a beautiful plant! They are among my favorites. The sedum autumn fire plant is one of my favorite perennial plants. We have a few clusters planted in various areas in our backyard and enjoy them from spring to the fall months. I'm in awe as I closely observe these plants. Each cluster is saturated with hundreds of tiny star-shaped petal-type flowers. They are a yellowish, light green in the spring, then turn a maroon-ish color as the buds open in early fall.

Pollinators love these plants, and they attract butterflies. They make excellent cut flower arrangements and bloom for a long time. They are rabbit resistant and perfect for use on yard slopes. They love full sun and are draught tolerant.

Sedum autumn fire plant
(Photo by the author)

Cut sedum autumn fire plants back in early spring, and new growth will emerge. They can be divided in the spring to plant in other areas. They don't require deadheading during the growing season. Pinch them back during early summer if height control is desired.

Soil

What is soil? Soil is composed of three different size mineral particles of sand, silt, and clay. The percentage of each determines its texture as well as physical properties. The ideal soil is called loam and consists of equal parts of sand, silt, and clay. Soil is "alive," whereby dirt is dead and lacks a living ecosystem. Soil is full of living organisms that help plants thrive. Soil is created when mountain stones and bedrock are broken down by wind and rain over centuries, with inputs from plants, animals, and bacteria. Using lime in the soil will decrease its pH while using sulfur will increase its pH. Rainfall is very effective in causing soils to become acidic, providing that a lot of rainwater rapidly moves through the soil. Sandy soils are often the first to become acidic because water percolates rapidly.

Spanish Moss

This humid thriving tree grows in the Southern United States, and the fragile stems are often used to stuff mattresses, automobile seats, furniture, home insulation, and for packing material. Spanish moss can also be used in floral arrangements and for mulch. Spanish moss may cause skin rash if not handled properly.

Spanish moss tree

Spanish moss is an air plant which can pull moisture from the air. It thrives in areas such as rivers and ponds. Although they are akin to pineapples trees, Spanish moss is not edible. Many wildlife animals use the moss to hide from predators. Several species of bats use Spanish moss for daytime resting places. Spanish moss is used by birds for nesting material. They prefer high light and use declining trees as a place for the moss. It is unlikely to get chiggers from moss hanging on the trees as chiggers are found on the ground so you could get them if we come in contact with the ground moss.

Tomatoes

Remove the "sucker" growth between the main stem and the tomato branch to promote growth. Suckers can draw energy away from the main stems, thus reduce healthy tomato growth.

Tomato sucker middle stem
(Photo by the author)

Trees

Tree Type	Tree Identification
Balsam Fir	3/4 to 1 1/4 inch needles.
Balsam Poplar	Leaves are finely toothed
Beech	Leaves are shiny and leathery, coarse, sharp teeth
Big-toothed Aspen	Leaves have large teeth
Black Ash	9 to 11 leaflets without petioles
Black Cherry	Fine blunt teeth, leaves 2 to 6 inches long, dark bark
Black Locust	Rounded leaflets
Black Spruce	1/3 to 3/4 inch needles, twigs have hair, grows in wet areas
Black Oak	Pointed lobes, deep sinuses, young hairy leaves
Black Walnut	Leaves are 8 to 24 inches
Box Elder	3 leaflets, rarely 5
Eastern Hemlock Needles	1/2 inch long
Eastern Red Cedar Berries	Scaly and prickly, rounded needles
Green Ash	7 to 9 leaflets with petiole
Jack Pine	2 needle clusters under 2 inches long
Mountain Ash	Pointed leaflets 6 to 8 inches long
Northern Pin Oak	Pointed lobes, deep sinuses extend 3/4 of the way to midvein, leaves hairless, bright green and shiny
Northern White Cedar Cone	Scales are flat, branches are fanlike
Pitch Pine	3 needle clusters, 3 to 4 inches long
Red Maple	Leaf edges double-toothed, 3 to 5 lobes
Red Pine	2 needle clusters, 3 to 4 inches long

Shagbark Hickory	7 leaflets or less, usually 5, egg-shaped nut
Silver Maple	Leaf edges single-toothed, 3 to 5 lobes, lobes are separated by deep angular openings
Sugar Maple	Leaf edges are smooth, 5 lobes
Tamarack	More than 5 needle clusters
Trembling Aspen	Leaves have small, fine teeth about 1/16 inch
Weeping Willow	Leaves are 3 times as long as its width
White Ash	5 to 9 leaflets, smile-shaped
White Birch	Leaves single-toothed, white peeling bark
White Oak	Lobes rounded, leaves 5 to 9 inches long hairless, deep sinuses
White Pine	5 needle clusters 2 to 3 inches long, need shade to grow
White Spruce	1/3 to 3/4 inch needles, twigs are hairless
Yellow Birch	Leaves double-toothed, dull green, yellow or bronzed bark

Sinuses are the outside edge of a leaf that turns toward the leaf center then back to the edge, leaving leaf lobes on each side. Petiole is the stock that attaches a leaf to its stem. Lobe and teeth are similar. Lobes are outer sections of a leaf that extend outward from its mid-vein by greater than 1/4 of an inch, whereby a tooth is less than 1/4 of an inch.

Tulips

Tulips are wildflowers and are native to Central Asia. The word "tulip" comes from the Persian word meaning "turban." Holland's tulip industry began in the 1500s, and today, Holland is the largest producer of tulips in the world. Holland produces over four billion tulip bulbs annually, with half that amount exported.

Each color of tulip has the following significance:

1. Red for love and romance.
2. White to convey an apology.
3. Purple is associated with royalty.
4. Yellow for cheer and happiness.

Plant tulips in the fall before the ground freezes. They do best in the sun or partial shade with fertile, neutral pH soil. If the soil is too soggy, bulbs will rot, so make sure the soil drains well. Dig a hole about three times the size of the bulb. Smaller bulbs can be planted four inches below the surface while larger bulbs should be planted six to eight inches below the surface and four to five inches apart. Set the bulbs in with the pointed end up. Fill the hole, pat it down, then water thoroughly.

Tulips are the national flower of both Iran and Turkey. Tulips follow the sun even when they're in a vase. That's why it's important to move or rotate them around during different times of the day. Tulips continue to grow after they have been cut. Cut tulips after blossom are gone.

Wintergreen Plant

The wintergreen plant will not reproduce after its soil has been plowed. Therefore, evidence of wintergreen plants in an area suggest that its soil was never plowed.

Wintergreen plant
Author: Agnieszka Kwiecień
This photo is subject to a Creative Commons License
https://creativecommons.org/licenses/by-sa/4.0/deed.en
No changes were made to this photo.

The bright red berries found on wintergreen plants remain on the plant all winter long and provides nourishment for many species of birds as well as other wildlife animals. The wintergreen plant is an excellent evergreen ground cover. This plant prefers shade to semi-shade, with moist, acidic soils.

Once established, the wintergreen plant can withstand drought and excessive heat. The wintergreen bell-shaped white flowers blossom in early summer, and they then turn to their familiar red berries. The leaves turn a deep purple in the fall. The oils from the leaves produce a mint aroma, as well as used in medicine to produce anti-inflammatory remedies.

Chapter 5
Warm-Blooded vs. Cold-Blooded

Introduction

As with all humans, warm-blooded creatures, such as birds and animals, generate their body heat by converting the food they eat into energy. They need to keep the inside of their bodies at a temperature relative to other species. However, when warm-blooded creatures become too warm due to excessive activity or when they are in a warm environment, they sweat or pant to expel their excessive heat through water evaporation. Conversely, when they are in a cold environment, they have various means to keep warm within the different species.

Cold-blooded animals, on the other hand, such as snakes, insects, fish, alligators, frogs, turtles, spiders, and reptiles, cannot regulate their body temperatures because they don't have sweat glands or any other means to cause evaporation. Therefore, their body temperature changes with the environment they are in. Some animals, like the mako shark and the great white shark, are partially warm-blooded. The body temperature of these animals can raise about the same temperature of their surrounding water.

I have researched data about creatures, such as insects, birds, mammals, and animals, that I found to be very interesting and a valuable source for my thought concept. Simply thinking about their everyday challenges, extraordinary behavior, and difficult survival methods these creatures must endure was the inspiration to include "Thoughts from Warm-Blooded" and "Thoughts from Cold-

Blooded" in the following chapters in this book. Although many of us are aware of the topics discussed, I found that a steady reminder not only reinforces our awareness but at the same time provides the power and incentive to think positively. "Knowledge is power."

How much do we really know about animals and insects? How much do we even care to know? As an animal lover, and with a deep interest and respect for these creatures, I thought it would be helpful to share some knowledge and interesting facts with my readers. With only a few exceptions, animals and birds are warm-blooded while reptiles, insects, and fish are cold-blooded. The temperature of a creature's blood is related to its body temperature. So then what does it mean to be warm-blooded? And what does it mean to be cold-blooded?

A word about nocturnal and diurnal. Animals are generally classified as either diurnal (belonging to the day) or nocturnal (belonging to the night), referring to the time of day whereby various species exhibit different behaviors when closest to their preferred temperature cycle and comfort zone. One of the most important factors contributing to this pattern is their vision's ability to collect light. By their nighttime and daytime feeding and activity needs, diurnal and nocturnal animals occupy and control their areas, thus maintaining a natural wildlife balance.

Diurnal animals have a lower body temperature suited for the warmth of the daytime sun while the temperature of nocturnal animals is adapted to cooler nights. The differences maximize the efficiency of their metabolism. Each type of animal has adjusted to its environment for survival. Both types of animals communicate in various ways, ultimately depending on its needs within the surroundings which it lives.

Although nocturnal and diurnal animals have dissimilar habits, there are nevertheless some dramatic overlaps. Many habits encompass both night and day, depending on the situation. For example, many birds are diurnal but may also be busy with a variety of activities during dawn and at dusk. Similarly, many rodents are nocturnal but may also feed during the day if there is a necessity and little predator risk. Whether an animal is nocturnal or diurnal depends highly on many factors, including hunger, survival, shelter, and predators.

Diurnal

Diurnal animals and creatures are generally active during the daytime then rest during the night. They have good daytime vision but poor night vision. Diurnal animals generally have smaller eyes, which allow them to handle brighter levels of light during the day due to the high density of cone cells in their retina, which allows them to see colors and details in bright light. Diurnal animals share information with one another through body, language, or scent and rely on visual cues for communications. Some examples of diurnal animals include guinea pigs, rabbits, chipmunks, hawks, cows, elephants, squirrels, eagles, sheep, and dogs.

Nocturnal

Approximately 75 percent of all animals are of the nocturnal species. Nocturnal animals and creatures are primarily active during the nighttime hours, then they conserve energy during the day by resting and being less active. Nocturnal animals typically have better hearing, smell, and large sensitive eyes with a few to no cone cells in their retina. They also have a reflective area behind their retina, which increase light levels during night use. These types of animals rely on touch or taste to communicate with one another as well as sounds and calls.

Some nocturnal species include cockroaches, owls, skunks, badgers, leopards, bedbugs, tigers, lions, frogs, gerbils, rats, mice, raccoons, snails, foxes, armadillos, hamsters, crickets, alligators, scorpions, and hermit crabs.

Crepuscular and matutinal

Other types of animal behavior include the crepuscular species, which are generally active during dusk and twilight hours. Examples include barn owls, moths, moles, deer, bobcats, groundhogs, ferrets, and black bear. Animals that are more active during early morning or at predawn, such as hunting, eating, and mating, are considered matutinal animals and creators. Such animals may include bees, gerbils, rats, and other rodents.

Animal Diets

Here's a reminder of the diets of various animals:

- Herbivores—Animals that exclusively diets on plants, such as the mouse, deer, elks, elephants, giraffes, cows, and horses.
- Carnivores—Animals that exclusively diets on meat, such as the lions, tigers, wolves, snakes, crocodiles, eagles, seals, octopuses, sharks, and spiders.
- Omnivores—Animals that diet on both meat and plant, such as the humans, turtles, pigs, squirrels, bear, and foxes.

Part 1
Warm-Blooded

Advantages of being warm-blooded

Warm-blooded creatures can remain active and search for food in a wide range of temperatures and environments. The higher body temperatures of warm-blooded animals serve to optimize their immune system to withstand infections, further helping more animals to survive, and reproduce. They can live in almost any surface environment, such as in the arctic regions or on high-elevation mountains. They can defend themselves in a wide range of outdoor temperatures and environments.

Disadvantages of being warm-blooded

Animals that are too small will lose heat faster than they can produce it. Warm-blooded animals provide warm body environments to invite viruses, bacteria, and parasites. Warm-blooded animals must consume a lot of food to keep their normal body temperatures.

Animal Eyes

A membrane behind the retina of most warm-blooded nocturnal animals reflects incoming light back to the rods in the eye to increase the amount of light absorbed, and thus the reason they are able to see much better in the darkness.

Anteaters

Anteaters need to consume an average of about thirty-five thousand ants and termites every night. They have a life span between two and fourteen years in the wild, depending on the species. However, the giant anteater can live to twenty-six years.

Giant anteater are about seven feet long, including its tail. Silky anteater are about fourteen inches long. Southern tamandua and northern tamandua anteaters are over three feet long.

All anteaters have elongated snouts equipped with a thin tongue that can be extended to a length greater than the length of its head. Their tube-shaped mouths have lips but no teeth. They are fed on small insects. Their dense and long fur protects them from insect attacks. The tongue is covered with thousands of tiny hooks which are used to hold the insects together with large amounts of saliva.

The anteater uses its sharp claws to tear an opening into anthills and insert their long snout and efficient tongue to work. Their long tongues are capable of lapping up nearly thirty-five thousand ants and termites whole each day. Although they flick their tongues up to 160 times per minute, they need to feast quickly because the ants fight back with painful stings. Anteaters also eat soft bodied grubs, soft fruits, and bird eggs.

Anteaters have poor sight, good hearing, and excellent sense of smell. All anteaters are mainly nocturnal; however, the giant anteater can also be active during the day. Female anteaters give birth to a single baby. Gestation period is between 120 to 190 days. Little anteater stays with mother for two years or until she becomes pregnant again. Mother carries her baby on her back during the first year. Anteaters typically sleep up to fifteen hours per day.

The main predators of anteaters are pumas, jaguars, and humans. Anteaters are not aggressive, but they can be fierce. A cornered anteater will rear up on its hind legs, using its tail for balance, and lash out with dangerous claws. The giant anteater's claws are about four inches long and can even kill their predators. The tongue of a giant anteater can extend over two feet to capture their prey. With a body temperature fluctuating between 91°F and 97°F, anteaters have among the lowest body temperatures of any mammal. Anteaters are very careful to avoid the dangerous and aggressive soldier ant. A group of anteaters is called a parade. Anteaters are closely related to sloths and armadillos.

Armadillos

Nine-banded armadillos cannot coil up like three-banded armadillos can. Nine-banded can postpone pregnancy up to three years to avoid droughts and disasters, and they produce multiple quadruplets. Of the twenty different types of armadillos in North and South America, only nine-banded armadillo calls the US their home. Nine-banded armadillos, however, can have anywhere from seven to eleven bands on its shell. Armadillos have terrible eyesight but excellent sense of smell as well as strong legs and very sharp claws. These peaceful mammals, typically no bigger than the size of a small dog, use their powerful noses to look for food at night.

Armadillos enjoy warm, wet environments, which is why they stick mostly to the southern states. Most enjoy forests and grasslands, and since they can hold their breath for about six minutes, they have no problem crossing a river or a stream or walking along the bottom of a stream. Armadillos burrow underground and sleep for up to sixteen hours. They often have multiple burrows situated around their hunting grounds, but they aren't territorial and have no problem leaving their burrow to find better feeding areas. Their abandoned burrows often host other animals, such as snakes, skunks, and rodents.

After dusk, armadillos leave their underground home to hunt for food. Their diet typically consists of insects, such as termites, beetles, grubs, scorpions, and cockroaches, just to name a few. They also eat plants, small reptiles, and their eggs. Armadillos are not aggressive. However, unless you are trying to catch one, it's unlikely an armadillo will cause any problems. Armadillos are surprisingly fast.

Armadillos live anywhere from seven to twenty years. Armadillos give birth once a year and always to a litter of four males or four females. Only two types of armadillos can roll themselves into a ball, the Brazilian armadillo and the southern three-banded armadillo. Both are found in South America. Armadillos are the only mammal with a hard shell.

Bats

Bats are the only mammals capable of sustaining flight. Other mammals known to fly can only glide for short distances. Bats do not flap their entire forelimbs as birds do, but instead, they flap their spread-out digits, which are very long and covered with a thin membrane. Most bats pollinate flowers as well as disperse fruit seeds. In fact, many tropical plants depend entirely on the bat population for the distribution of their seeds. Bats that consume insects reduce the need for pesticides.

When bats fly erratically toward and around your head, they are not attacking you. They are simply hunting for mosquitoes and other insects drawn to your body heat. About 70 percent of bat species are insect eaters or insectivores while about 30 percent are a combination of fruit eaters, fish eaters, or vampire bats, which exclusively feed on blood of other animals. Hawks, eagles, and snakes are major predators of vampire bats.

Here are some steps to prevent bats from entering your home:

1. Seal all exterior openings with caulk or screen material.
2. Install caulking or weather stripping around all windows and doors.

Bat hibernation

Bats cannot maintain a constant body temperature, so they either migrate to warmer climates during cold winter months or they search for a place to hibernate such as in dark and secluded places, like hollow trees, barns, or empty buildings, when their food sources are no longer available. However, bat species that migrate follow a seasonal migration pattern. They cool off when they are not active. During hibernation, the heartbeat of a bat slows down from as high as 200 to 300 beats per minute to as low as 10 beats per minute, which allows them to survive for up to six months on their stored body fat. They lose as much as half their body weight during hibernation and can lower their body temperature from about 100 degrees to about 40 degrees to preserve energy. By spring, bats would typically have lost approximately half of their body weight. Most bat species can enter any building through openings as small as 1/4 of an inch!

Bat droppings

Bat droppings are dry and black in color and approximately the size of a grain of rice. Bat droppings accumulate and become evident under areas where bats roost.

Bat navigation

Bats use of their ultrasonic echolocation (sonar) capabilities but are severely interfered by unwanted echoes from background noise, such as moving vehicles. Their sonar only works at short ranges; therefore, bats use their vision for detection of landmarks and to avoid colliding with objects while in flight.

Bats also rely on their memory as they often follow the same paths every night. Although the eyes of bats are small, they are well adapted for low illumination, having mainly rod-based retinas, lenses, and generally large receptors. Bats can easily detect small variations in brightness. When commuting between their roost and feeding locations during dusk and dawn periods, bats often follow outlines of landscapes. The reason may be to minimize risk from predators or to use outlines as acoustic landmarks, which perhaps facilitate navigation by sonar.

However, landscape outlines and silhouettes provide bats with visual cues, contrasting against the twilight sky, and such cues are probably essential for orientation and navigation along traveling routes. Bats trust their eyes over their ears when exposed to contradictory auditory and visual challenges. When released indoors, bats have a tendency to crash into windows of buildings. This suggests that they predominantly rely on their vision rather than on their echolocation. However, there are fewer collisions when bats are blinded or when they fly under dark conditions and forced to rely on echolocation alone.

Bat orientation

When moving toward resting places and specific sites, bats face unfavorable conditions for orientation, such as darkness, acoustic clutter, and calls from other bats. Therefore, their memory is of great importance. Bats can remember positions of narrow openings with an accuracy of less than one inch. If an obstacle is removed from their flight path, bats may continue to avoid that position for days. However, bats do not completely trust their memory but can compare stored data with new sound and visual information. Under dark conditions, bats may still be able to see insects. For example, bat activity is high where fireflies occur, and it has been shown that some fireflies stop flashing when approached by bats, suggesting that the light they emit evoke bat curiosity. Fruit- and nectar-feeding bats have larger eyes than insectivorous bats.

Vampire bats

Like ordinary bats, vampire bats also hang by their feet while sleeping. However, unlike ordinary bats who cross their wings (hands), vampire bats hang their hands straight downward.

Bears

Bears hibernate during the winter, and during hibernation, they live off stored body fat. They can drop their body temperatures by as much as 10°F to 15°F. Starting early winter, bear metabolism lowers, thus reducing the need to eat much. Bears do not urinate or defecate during winter, and they do not completely hibernate. Bears wake up during hibernation to move around inside its den.

Grizzly bears

Brown bears are synonymous with grizzly bears. Bears that live inland are called grizzly bears while those living on the coast are referred to as brown bears. Their smell is seven times more powerful than that of the average dog. Grizzly bears have no natural enemies.

Polar bears

The skin of polar bears is actually black so it can absorb up as much of the sun's rays as possible for warmth. Polar bears have almost transparent fur over their black skin. Reflection of the sunlight from the densely packed transparent hairs makes polar bears appear to be white. The seemingly transparent fur is made up of hollow hairs called guard hairs. These air-filled guard hairs help transmit heat from the sunlight to the polar bear's black skin as a solar heat collector. In turn, the reflection stops the heat being lost from their black skin, similar to a greenhouse effect.

The polar bear can swim in icy seawater very comfortably. They are more in danger of hyperthermia or overheating then hypothermia or freezing. Polar bears can be found in the northern hemisphere

Canada, Alaska, Russia, Greenland, Norway, and specifically, the Artic Pole. Polar bears do not exist in Antarctica.

Birds

Arctic terns

These birds make the longest journey of all animals, flying approximately twenty-five thousand miles each year.

Bald eagles

The bald eagle was selected as the national bird of the United States in 1782. The population of this magnificent bird dropped drastically in the late 1900s due to the use of pesticides, hunting by humans, and pollution of rivers. However, a successful recovery plan was created by the US government, which removed the bald eagle from the endangered species list.

It has a wingspan of five to eight feet. Its length is twenty-eight to thirty-eight inches from head to tail. Bald eagles weigh 6 1/2 to 14 pounds. Some are migrant. They live near water, including rivers, lakes, and coastal locations with altitudes of approximately 6,500 feet.

Differences between male and female bald eagles. Female bald eagles are larger in size, and their wingspans are longer. Also, their back talon is longer, and she has a bigger and longer beak. The beak may even start behind her eye as compared to the beak of a male bald eagle.

What do bald eagles look like? Adult bald eagle are unmistakably recognized by their prominent white head, yellow eyes, beak, and feet that contrast against the dark brown of its wings and back. The juvenile's plumage is not as recognizable as adults and at times can be mistaken for a golden eagle. The juvenile bald eagle develops into its full adult plumage at about four years of age.

Winter-feeding bald eagles. During the winter, large numbers of bald eagles gather at the site of spawning grounds of salmon. These bald eagles compete against other predatory birds and grizzly bears for the dead and dying salmon fish.

What is a pip hole on a bald eagle? A pip hole is a tiny hole that the unborn eaglet makes through his shell with its "egg tooth" (a sharp small point at the end of its beak) when it begins to hatch.

Eaglet's first flight. The time frame before baby eaglet begin to fly is about ten to thirteen weeks after they hatch.

Steller's sea eagles

Steller's sea eagles are found in Russia's Kamchatka Peninsula. When food is scarce, Steller's sea eagles will fight to the death.

Hummingbirds

Hummingbirds travel thousands of miles mainly for food. They cross the Atlantic Ocean, around South America, then go back home. The going route is different than the return route. During the going route, they take advantage of the trade winds while during the return route, they take advantage of food supply.

Here are some facts about hummingbirds:

- Length is about 3 3/4 inches.
- Weigh less than three paper clips.
- Average hummingbird wings beat about 50 to 70 times per second.
- Heart rate when sleeping is about 50 to 180 beats per minute.
- Normal heart rate is about 1,360 beats per minute.
- Body temperature is about 109°F.
- Eats about fifteen times every hour to survive.
- Can starve to death in two hours.
- Natural enemy is the praying mantis.
- The only bird that can hover, fly backward and up or down.
- They can perch, but they cannot walk.
- Nest made from plant material and spider webs.

- Nest is about 5 to 20 feet above ground.
- After mating, female builds nest and raises young.
- Incubation is about twenty days by the mother.
- Young will leave the nest twenty to twenty-two days after hatching.
- Territory about 1/4 acre.
- Dives in U shape, rising 10 to 40 feet on each side.
- Typically fly about 25 MPH, and up to 50 MPH.
- Burns approximately 155,000 calories per day.
- Diet includes nectar and insects.
- They are the smallest bird in the world.
- Average life span is three to four years.
- They open their beaks wide during flight to catch insects.

Many hummingbirds migrate to the South in the fall and spend winter in Mexico or Central America. Hummingbirds are so smart they can remember every flower and feeder they have ever visited as well as how long it will take for certain flowers to refill with nectar.

Osprey

Unlike most birds of prey, ospreys are tolerant of human activities and will build nests on almost any suitable structure close to water that has an abundant supply of fish. Utility poles and man-made poles are favorite nesting locations.

Identifying ospreys. Osprey is dark brown above, white below, with white head and prominent dark eye stripe. In flight, crooked wings are distinctive. Their white bottom blends with clouds, thus fooling the fish below. Their call is a series of loud and sharp whistles.

Beneficial coexistence with ospreys. Ospreys live in close proximity to humans. They can warn us of harmful environmental conditions in and near our communities and alert us of the abundance of fish activity in the oceans. We can return the favor by making the environment safer for osprey birds, construct and maintain safe nesting platforms, and keep our waters clean. This sort of coexistence between wildlife and humans contributes to our survival as well as that of other species on the planet.

Here are some osprey characteristics:

- Osprey's weight is about 2.5 to 4.5 pounds, with wingspan of about 56 inches.
- An average-sized osprey nest can weigh as much as forty pounds and is approximately forty inches in diameter.
- The quantities of osprey eggs are from one to four, but three is average. Egg colors are creamy white, slightly larger than chicken eggs, and heavily blotched with dark brown. The eggs hatch in about thirty-eight days.
- The osprey diet is about 99 percent fish. Ospreys are able to catch fish by hovering above the water and then plunging up to three feet into the water feet first using specially designed foot pads for grasping slippery fish. Their dense, oily feathers make them well suited to rapidly repel water and quickly regain momentum in flight.
- Maximum life span is approximately twenty-five years in the wild.
- The male osprey brings fish to the female throughout the incubation and nestling periods and also shares a portion of the duties. The female remains in constant contact with her chicks until they are about forty days old. She then leaves the nest often to perch nearby. She occasionally shares hunting duties with the male until the chicks are able to fly at about the age of fifty days.
- Adult osprey pairs migrate separately during winter at different locations, reuniting each spring at their original nest after being away for six months.

Ospreys are biological indicators. Why are ospreys good biological health indicators of the ecosystem? About 99 percent of their diet is fish captured near the nest site. Each pair of ospreys mate for life and returns to the same nest annually. Single nests are often distributed at regular intervals along rivers and sometimes in colonies near estuaries with abundant fish populations. They often build large, visible nests on accessible structures. They tolerate short-term disturbance at their nest site. These traits allow researchers to quickly locate nests at these sites.

Use of artificial osprey nest sites. Ospreys generally build their nests on potentially dangerous wiring on the top of utility poles. Utility companies must, therefore, develop several plans to resolve power outages and electrocution problems while still accommodating nesting osprey. Their actions include building an alternate nesting platform above the power pole wires. Some osprey nests obstruct waterway navigational channel marker lights. The US Coast Guard is accommodating ospreys by constructing platforms nests away from channel marker lights.

Owls

Owls cannot smell and, therefore, are not bothered by skunks. Owl ears are aft of their eyes and covered with feathers. Some owl ears are not level with each other, which enables acute stereoscopic hearing, allowing sounds to arrive into one ear microseconds before the other, and helps the owl to locate its prey. Because of feathered wing structure, owls do not create noise while flying.

Penguins

There aren't any penguins on the North Pole or in the northern hemisphere. All nineteen species of penguins are found below the equator in the southern hemisphere, such as in New Zealand, Australia, and primarily in Antarctica.

Cats

Cats eat grass for medicinal purposes, such as an upset stomach, for example. Eating grass makes cats regurgitate fur balls or foreign objects inside their stomachs that are hard or impossible to digest, such as bones. It would be safer for cats to throw it up rather than pass it out through the opposite end. Therefore, cats always need to have access to grass. Cats do not eat grass for its nutrients.

Female cats seem to be "right-handed" as they generally lead with their right paw.

Ancient Egyptians believed cats were capable of bringing good luck to those who housed and took care of them. Those with wealth would honor cats by dressing them in jewels and feeding them treats that were fit for royalty. When cats died, they were mummified. Although cats were not worshipped as gods, they were chosen by the gods as messengers and for their likeness. Cats reminded ancient Egyptians the power of the gods.

Misty
Photo by the author

Some interesting facts about cats:

- Cats have sweat glands on their feet.
- They have no ability to taste sweet things.
- They have one of three blood types.
- Have approximately six times better vision in the dark than humans.

- Their claws are curled inward. Climbing trees is easy but impossible climbing down.
- Cats do not have a collarbone, so they can fit through anywhere their head can fit.

Cat food

Use of corn, wheat, or soy can cause skin irritation, dental issues, loss of fur, fever, ear infections, kidney and liver failure, obesity, chronic digestive issues, and heart disease. Since cat food manufacturers ensure that dry cat foods have a twelve-month shelf life in order to remain edible through shipping and storage, the fats used in the foods are preserved with synthetic or natural preservatives. Animal by-products are ingredients not fit for human consumption, such as floor sweepings. Pet foods containing animal by-products must include the words "meal" or "by-product" on the ingredients label.

Inedible by-products, such as bone, fat, heads, hair, feet, and internal organs, are used in commercial pet food. These materials are sent for processing into pet food products. When the source of the meat is known it will be listed as beef, poultry, chicken, turkey, etc. If the source is unknown, it will be listed as "meat." Animals from research laboratories may be used for pet food as well. The life span of your cat should be approximately thirteen to twenty years.

Algonquin cat

They are often called "rag cats." They are approximately three times bigger than all other domestic cats. They have blue oval eyes, pointed ears and tails, and are relatively easy to groom.

Calico cats

Calico cats have short hair and are any breed that have tricolors (generally, 75 percent white, with orange and black patches). An extremely high percentage of calico cats are female. They require minimal grooming. They live for approximately fifteen to twenty years. The calico cat is the state cat for Maryland (the coon cat for Maine). Calico cats are considered as good luck cats in Japan. Japanese sailors would even travel with calico cats for protection.

Persian cats

They are the most popular and longest hair of all domestic cats. Some craftsmen shave then spin Persian cat hair to make expensive handbags, selling up to several hundred dollars. Persian cats live for approximately fifteen to twenty years and must be groomed about every six weeks. Persian cats, however, are prone to disease.

Savannah cats

Savannah cats are the largest and wildest of all domestic cat breeds. However, they are loyal and will follow their owners around the house. They can be trained to walk on a leash and to fetch as well.

Sphynx cats

They are the least popular of all domestic cats. They appear to have no hair but actually have a layer of fuzz over their body. Sphynx cats are strong and relatively medium in size. The pigment in their skin determines their color. They have wide ears, oval paws, and large slanted eyes. They have no health issues. Lack of hair leaves their skin free of oils. Their metabolism requires constant food, and they always want to be the center of attention.

Camels

Camels have two rows of long eyelashes and a third eyelid, which acts like a windshield wiper to wash away sand, dust, and dirt from their eyes. Their nostrils can close to protect them from airborne sand. Their broad, flat feet have two toes with leathery pads on each of their four feet, which helps prevent them from sinking into sand. Camels have the ability to go for weeks without water. They can handle extreme dehydration. They have been known to safely lose body water equivalent to 40 percent of its body weight, a loss that would be lethal in any other animal. How do they do this?

Camels can take in a very large amount of water during one session to make up for previous fluid loss. In other animals, this would result in severe problems. Camels can do this because water is absorbed very slowly from their stomach and intestines, allowing time to establish a balance. Furthermore, their blood cells can swell to about 240 percent of normal size without bursting. (Other species can only increase to about 150 percent.)

Their kidneys are capable of concentrating their urine to reduce water loss. Their urine can become as thick as syrup and have twice the salt content of seawater. They can extract water from their fecal pellets immediately after voiding to be used for energy. A camel has the ability to have large temperature fluctuations from 97.7°F to 107.6°F. During the day, its body tends to repel heat, and during cool desert nights, their heat is dissipated. This makes them useful pack animals across deserts.

One- or two-hump camels?

Some believe that humps are used to store water, but camels' humps actually store fatty tissue used for a source of nourishment when food becomes scarce. Camel humps depend on the species. One-hump camels are found in North Africa, Arabia, and the Middle East. Two-hump camels are shorter and heavier and are found in Central Asia, Mongolia, and China.

Chicken

Chicken eggs are laid having a natural bloom covering, which protects the egg against bacteria from getting through the pours of the shell. Slightly brushed eggs can be packaged and unrefrigerated for several weeks. Once out of the fridge, condensation will form and remove the bloom. Eggs must, therefore, remain in the fridge until used. Washing, however, will remove the bloom, and the eggs must then be refrigerated immediately.

Chipmunks

Chipmunks prefers open deciduous woodlands, forest edges, brushy areas, stone walls, and around houses. Chipmunks are ground-dwelling mammals, digging tunnels or burrows about two inches in diameter. Entrance to their tunnel system is typically next to a solid object, such as tree stumps or large rocks. Secondary exits are often in open areas, and there are no dirt piles around the hole. This makes it difficult for predators to find. The chipmunk digs with its front paws, each with four sharp claws. The dirt is push to the surface and then carried away in the animals' cheeks.

The tunnel system can be as long as thirty feet in length, with several interconnecting passages. Tunnels are normally two to three feet below ground. Most burrows have several sleeping areas as well as food storage areas. The sleeping areas are made larger and filled with shredded leaves to make comfortable beds. Food is normally stored in the lowest tunnels to keep it cool, dry, and fresh. Chipmunks have soft feet with nails on each toe that enables them to climb well as they can wrap their feet around things. They have four toes on their two front feet and five toes on their two back feet, which gives them more stability when standing on their back feet. This arrangement is very similar to mice.

Here are the eight things to know about chipmunks:

1. Chipmunks are basically tiny squirrels about 1 to 5 ounces.
2. North America is home to about twenty-one chipmunk species.
3. Chipmunks produce one or two litters a year. Young are on their own within eight weeks.
4. Chipmunks prefer forest areas.
5. They eat various types of seeds as well as fungus, helping to spread the fungi that live around tree roots and are critical

to tree survival. Chipmunks also spread the seeds of trees and other plants.

6. Chipmunks aren't particularly choosy about what they eat. Along with seeds and fungi, they eat grain, fruit, nuts, insects, worms, bird eggs, and even nestling birds and baby mice.

7. Chipmunks recognize three different calls: the chip, the deeper chuck, and the startle call. The startle call is an alarm that warns of imminent danger. Chipmunks will make calls in a chorus of several chipmunks.

8. Chipmunks in the wild live for two to three years and longer in captivity.

Anatomy of the chipmunk

The chipmunk is reddish brown on top, with white belly fur. It has one white stripe boarded by two black stripes, starting at the side of the head and continuing to the rump. These stripes are parallel and on both sides of the body. It has two lighter white stripes down the back, which are much thinner than the side stripes. The tail is brown, with varied shades of black near the end. The ears are small and face forward. The eyes are small and set on the sides of the head.

The head tapers to a point at the mouth. The chipmunk's mouth is small, but its cheeks can expand to three times its head size. An adult chipmunk is 8 1/2 to 11 1/2 inches in length. Its tail is approximately four inches in length. The widest part of the body is around the shoulder area, about 1 1/2 inches across. The adult chipmunk weighs approximately 2 1/2 to 5 ounces.

Mating chipmunks

Mating occurs in early spring, and there is one litter per year. An average of three to five young are born in May. There have been reported litters as large as ten. The chipmunk is a social animal, in that both the male and female raise their young. There is very little to no difference between male and female chipmunks.

Chipmunk hibernation

Chipmunks hibernate from late fall to early spring, waking to eat every two weeks or so. They may occasionally appear on the surface during the winter but will not stay long especially if there is snow on the ground. Chipmunks will climb a tree to harvest acorns, hickory nuts, and hazelnuts, but they are not as agile in the trees as their squirrel cousins. The chipmunk prefers to find food on the ground whenever possible. The chipmunk spends almost its entire day searching and storing food. Generally, this is done from sunrise to sunset, and it is not unusual for them to harvest a bushel of nuts in a three-day period.

Although chipmunks are herbivorous, they will also eat small vertebrates, such as snails or slugs. It does not, however, search out this type of meal but will feast on them occasionally. Chipmunks in an urban environment will take handouts from humans. This can include a wide variety of foods from pastries to pizza. They do not store these types of foods, but they do seem to enjoy the novelty of human food. A chipmunk in the wild can live up to seven years. Many chipmunks will die during their first year due to lack of food or poor planning for the winter storage. Young chipmunks may come to the surface without thinking about the predators that may be waiting for them and end up as dinner.

The chipmunks' primary enemies are foxes, weasels, bobcats, badgers, and snakes. Birds, such as hawks, eagles, and owls, can take many chipmunks on the run over open ground. House cats are very successful hunters in urban areas and can be considered the chipmunks' worst enemies. Chipmunks communicate by both sounds and gestures. Their vocabulary is not large, with about thirty distinguishable combinations.

These can be loud, shrill "chip-chip-chip" sounds to the softer and slower "chuck-chuck" sounds. When combined with body gestures, such as tail waving, they can effectively communicate with other chipmunks.

Deer

Deer don't like to eat needles or bark of white pine trees, but instead, they love to eat poison ivy. A deer's diet consists of a variety of crops, grasses, vegetation, acorns, and nuts. A healthy deer will have a diverse diet with a variety of foods. Every day, a deer needs to eat about 6 to 8 percent of its body weight in green foliage to stay healthy. Feeding backyard deer carbohydrate-rich foods, like fruit, grains, and corn, can cause serious health problems as these foods are normally not part of their natural diet.

Dogs

The chow is the only dog that has a black tongue; all other dogs have pink tongues. Dogs have sweat glands only on their feet and have thirteen different blood types within the various species, of which eight blood types are international standards. Dogs eat grass when they have an upset stomach. The grass makes them regurgitate fur balls or things that are hard to digest, like bones etc. It is safer for dogs to throw it up rather than allow it to pass through their digestive system. They do not eat grass for nutrients only for medical purposes. Therefore, dogs always need to have access to grass. My very best friend, Daisy, has created so many positive thoughts for me that she left no room for any negative thoughts.

Daisy
Photo by the author

Dogs that do not shed

Until I did some research, I did not realize that there were so many breeds of dogs that do not shed. I have listed dog breeds that have hair instead of fur and that do not shed much or not at all in alphabetical order:

- Basenji
- Beagle
- Bearded Collies
- Bedlington Terrier
- Bergamasco Poodle
- Bichon Frise
- Bolognese
- Border Terrier

- Boxer
- Brussels Griffon
- Chinese Crested
- Cotton de Tulear
- Dachshund
- French Bulldog
- Havanese
- Hungarian Puli
- Irish Water Spaniel
- Kerry Blue Terrier
- Lagotto Romagnolo
- Lhasa Apso
- Löwchen
- Maltese
- Poodle
- Portuguese Water Dog
- Schnauzer (miniature and standard)
- Shih Tzu
- Tibetan Terriers
- West Highland White Terrier
- Wire-Haired fox Terrier
- Xoloitzcuintli
- Yorkshire Terriers

Ducks

Males are exclusively called "drakes" while the term "duck" may refer to either gender. All ducks have highly waterproof feathers. Ducks are omnivorous and will eat grass, aquatic plants, insects, seeds, fruit, fish, crustaceans, and other types of food. Ducks are intelligent individuals who love spending their time relaxing on the water or searching for food. However, many of them don't have the opportunity to live the way they would like because humans kill them for their feathers and meat. Learn more about these remarkable animals and take a position to refuse ordering duck at restaurants or purchase duck meat or feather products.

These incredible swimmers have waterproof feathers, which have a waxy coating that protects an inner layer of down to keep them warm and dry. Their feet have blood vessels that are close together so they don't lose heat, and this allows them to swim in cold water without catching a chill. Some duck species can dive up to about forty feet into the water, and others can fly as high as four thousand feet in the air. Ducks can also fly long distances using the wind to help them reach speeds of up to 60 MPH.

Elephants

Elephants are the largest land animal in the world. They are almost fifteen feet high, weigh about fourteen thousand pounds, and can run around fifteen miles per hour. Elephants are found in Africa, South Asia, and Southeast Asia. They are herbivores animals. Their trunks are used for breathing, eating, drinking, and for taking dust baths. The elephant's brain is about eight pounds, which accounts for their amazing memory.

African elephants

African elephants have large ears, shaped much like the continent of Africa. They are warm-blooded, and their thin ears helps to dissipate heat quickly. They have fuller, more rounded heads, and the top of their head is a single dome.

Asian elephants

Asian elephants, on the other hand, have smaller ears and a twin domed head with an identifiable indentation in its center.

Fox

Our good friends Jack and Debbie of New Orleans, Louisiana, rescued Foxy when he was a baby then, in September 2010, released him into the wild after he was fully grown. It's so nice to have animal loving friends.

Frogs

Weather can be predicted 80 percent accurate by listening to the croaking of frogs. This formula was developed and used today by Chinese farmers. *If frog croaks on a fine day, it will rain in two days. If frog croaks after rain, fine weather coming. If frogs do not croak after successive overcast days, it will rain.*

Giraffes

Giraffes are interesting animals. They are found only in the eastern continent of Africa. They are the tallest land animals in the world with an average height of eighteen feet. They are herbivore animals, and they sleep while standing up for only about thirty minutes a day.

Groundhogs

Groundhogs are warm-blooded animals that hibernate in the winter. During hibernation, they live off stored body fat and can drop their body temperatures by as much as 50°F as well.

Horses

The height of a miniature horse is thirty-four inches or less. Any higher in size is considered a regular horse. The lime content in Kentucky soil is excellent for grass and thus nutritional for horses.

Mice

Mice do not hibernate. They store food in their burrows for winter. Mice have soft feet with nails on each of their toes that enables them to climb as well as wrap their toes around various objects. Mice have four toes on each of their two front feet and five toes on each of their two back feet which gives them more stability when standing on their back feet, similar to chipmunks.

Their life span is up to seven years. Their gestation period is twenty days. Mice weigh around 0.68 ounces. They are 3.9 inches long.

Mice are nocturnal and are always hungry. They become more active at night and are constantly looking for food. Mature mice range in age from three to six months. The eyesight of a mouse is not very good. They mainly rely on smell and feel through its whiskers and paws to navigate. They have an amazing sense of smell and hearing. A mouse can smell and feel tiny crumbs and other pieces of food lying around by sniffing and letting its whiskers drag on the floor or ground.

Mice are territorial. They make a nest and establish a territory around the nest. They will follow routines of checking around the perimeter of their territory, both to identify any predators, other mice, and to locate food. Once they use their senses to locate the best food sources within their territory, they will regularly revisit them. Mice communicate with one another about dangers as well as food sources via body language and high-pitched noises inaudible to humans.

Moles

Moles live underground, so the temperature of their environment does not change much. Moles are not rodents; they belong to the insectivores (insect eater) family and are found worldwide, except in Antarctica and South America. Moles have an extra thumb on each of their front hands, which helps them to dig. If you see a mole in your garden, don't think they are digging tunnels for a path to your vegetable roots. Instead, they are going after earthworms. They are hairless, have small eyes, a pointed snout, and their ears are tiny. Moles only weigh about four ounces but can grow to about seven inches long. These mammals come in various colors, such as orange, cream and white, or black.

They are not found in places where there's acidic soil or mountains but instead places where they can dig through soil to enjoy eating earthworms. Interesting enough, they keep earthworms alive by biting off their heads, which keeps them immobile. They then store the earthworms in chambers for a later feast. Males enlarge their tunnels during breeding season, then females give birth to three to four babies called pups. When the pups are about fourteen days old, they start to grow hair. At age five to six weeks, they leave their tunnel.

Some interesting things about moles:

- They eat their body weight in earthworms every day.
- Moles spend most of their time underground, but they are not blind. They see light and little movement.
- They use the scent sensors on their nose to find other moles and for food.
- Their tunnels include bedrooms, birthing areas, kitchens, and a means for traveling.
- They live in tunnels for generations until they decide to move.
- Moles enjoy living alone with only about four per acre.
- Their life span is about three years.
- Moles can live for eighteen minutes without oxygen.
- They are resistant to pain and rarely get cancer.
- Moles don't age.
- Moles have curved front paws that they use for digging through soil. They can dig up eighteen feet in about one hour.
- They don't hibernate. They're in search for food year-round.
- Moles have twice as much blood and more oxygen in their blood than any other mammal, which keeps them alive underground.
- Males are called boars while females are called sows.
- Moles provide soil aeration.
- They feast on slugs and creatures that eat plant roots.

Monkey

Finger Monkeys

The finger monkey is the smallest living monkey in the world but not the smallest primate. Finger monkeys are so small that they can hold on to your finger. They are also known as pocket monkeys. They are native to the rainforests of Brazil, Peru, Bolivia, Ecuador, and Colombia.

Moose

The flap under the throat of a moose is called a "bell." When their ears are back and the hair on their hump is raised and they are licking their lips, watch out…they will likely attack.

Here are a few interesting things about moose:

- Moose's life span is approximately up to twenty-five years.
- They can get as high as seven feet from the ground to their shoulders.
- Moose are herbivores. They have no upper teeth, but they have flat lower teeth for eating only plant material.
- Female moose weigh approximately 900 lbs. while male moose can weigh up to 1,500 lbs.
- Newborn moose weigh approximately thirty-three pounds.
- Moose can see well but only up to about twenty-five feet away.
- Moose can run about thirty-five miles per hour.

Muskrats

Muskrats are medium-sized rodents with an adaptable lifestyle and an omnivorous diet. They are much smaller than beavers with whom they often share their habitat. Their fur has two layers, which helps protect them from cold water. They have long tails covered with scales rather than hair and is used to aid them in swimming. Their tails are slightly flattened vertically, which is a shape that is unique to them. When they walk on land, their tails drag on the ground, which makes their tracks easy to recognize. Muskrats spend much of their time in the water and are well suited for their semiaquatic life.

Muskrats can swim under water for approximately ten to twenty minutes. Their bodies, like those of seals and whales, are less sensitive to the buildup of carbon dioxide than those of most other mammals. They can close off their ears to keep the water out. Their hind feet are semi webbed although while swimming, their tails are their main means of propulsion. They feed on cattails and other aquatic vegetation. Plant materials make up about 95 percent of their diets, but they also eat small animals, such as freshwater mussels, frogs, crayfish, fish, and small turtles. Females can have two or three litters a year of six to eight young. The babies are born small and hairless and weigh less than one ounce.

Panther

The panther, commonly known as black panthers, is a member of the big cat family native to Asia, the Americas, and Africa. The panther is not an actual species, but the name is generally used to refer to an all-black animal of the leopard and jaguar family. Gestation period is three months. Panthers spend their day relaxing on trees and hunting by night.

Possums

American's only marsupial (no placenta, and they develop inside their mother's pouch) animal. Possums are nature's sanitation engineers. They eat mice, rats, cockroaches, fruit, grain, berries, insects, snails, snakes, and anything you may not want around your home or yard. Babies are not attached to their mothers. Gestation period is about thirteen days. About twenty-five babies can be born at one time, each weighing 0.0046 pounds, and can all fit inside one teaspoon. However, mother can only support about thirteen babies.

At birth, the babies make their way into their mother's pouch then complete two months of development. They are solitary, nocturnal creatures and prefer to avoid confrontation. Their predators are foxes, coyotes, snakes, owls, hawks, dogs, and humans. They have no defense mechanisms except for a hiss, a show of their teeth, and they drool. Their body automatically shuts down when facing danger, thus the cliche "to play possum." The chances of possums having rabies are extremely rare. Possum life expectancy is approximately two years.

Primates

As with humans, apes, and monkeys, primates have sweat glands all over their bodies. The most important feature that distinguishes primates from other mammals is their brain. Monkeys, chimpanzees, and apes have larger-than-average brains compared to their body size. But why do they need bigger brains? To process the information required to effectively operate their thumbs, tails, and vision.

They are social mainly because they rely on their brains rather than their claws or teeth. Bigger brains also require time to develop. Newborns, for example, would not survive without the help of its parents. They seek the protection of their communities, similar to those of humans. However, not all primate communities are social. Murder and bullying are quite common. Some species will kill newborns.

Primates use tools more than any other type of animal. Also, like humans, most primates give birth to only one newborn at a time. Most species are omnivorous, feasting on fruits, leaves, insects, small lizards, and even mammals. However, tarsiers are the only primates entirely carnivorous while some are devoted vegetarians. Their preys include eagles, jaguars, and humans.

Rabbits

Rabbits are animals of the hare families. They resemble but are not related to the rodent family. Here are some differences between rabbits and hares:

Rabbits	Hares
Babies are born naked and blind.	Born with fur and vision.
Smaller than hares.	Larger than rabbits.
Shorter ears than hares.	Longer ears than rabbits.
Shorter hind legs.	Longer hind legs.
Their color is same every season.	Their color turns white in the winter.
Live together in colonies in burrows.	Do not live together. Females create flattened area called a "form" to deliver her young.

Rats

Rats are unable to regulate their body temperature; however, since they live underground, the temperature of their environment does not change much. Rats can survive longer without water than a camel can.

Rodents

What constitutes a rodent? Any relatively small placental mammal having large front teeth, which grow throughout their life. Rodents must constantly gnaw to prevent their teeth from growing too long. Rodents include rats, mice, porcupines, beavers, squirrels, naked mole rats, and hamsters.

Seagulls

Seagulls are creatures that mate for life (monogamous). They have a strong social structure that's effective against their predators. They have been known to gang up and drive intruders out to the ocean to drown.

Seagull
(Photo by the author)

Skunks

Skunks are nocturnal mammals. Their white stripe warns off predators, then if necessary, they stomp their feet, then they spray. The spray from a skunk takes a long time to manufacture; therefore, they spray only when absolutely necessary. They can spray up to fifteen feet away. However, after they spray three times, their system needs to refill their "pouches" Skunks dig holes while searching for grubs.

Squirrels

Squirrels are members of the small to medium-sized rodent family. The squirrel families include tree squirrels, ground squirrels, and flying squirrels. Squirrels are native to the America, Eurasia, and Africa. Except for tree squirrels, all squirrels hibernate during the winter season like chipmunks.

Here are some facts about squirrels:

- Predators are snake, coyote, weasel, bobcat, red-tailed hawk, northern goshawk, red fox, Arctic fox, herons, Cooper's hawk.
- Gestation period is anywhere from twenty-eight to forty-four days, depending on the specious.
- National Squirrel Appreciation Day is January 21.
- Squirrels can find food buried under one foot of snow.
- A squirrel's front teeth never stop growing. They must gnaw to control the length of their teeth. (Rodent is the Latin word for "gnaw.")
- Squirrels may lose as much as 25 percent of their buried food to thieves.
- Squirrels zig and zag to escape predators. This doesn't work well for cars, so please be careful!
- Squirrels may pretend to bury a nut to mislead potential thieves.
- A newborn squirrel is about an inch long.
- Humans introduced squirrels to most of our major city parks.
- Squirrels are acrobatic, intelligent, and adaptable.
- The nuts squirrels don't dig up results in more trees!

Turkeys

Benjamin Franklin suggested the wild turkey as our national bird. However, the turkey lost to the bald eagle by just one vote. Turkeys have extraordinary eyesight but cannot see well in the dark. Yes, turkeys are excellent flyers and can fly straight up to about fifty feet to roost and to sleep in low tree branches at night for protection from predators that roam at night. Turkeys then fly down at dawn to begin their new day. If they can't outrun a predator or if they can't run fast enough, they will just simply fly away at alarming speeds. They must be fast in order to capture their favorite food…insects.

Voles

Voles are similar to mice. However, they are usually smaller with stockier legs, shorter tails, and some have small hidden ears. Voles also have very small eyes, short snouts, and typically brownish in color with pale cream to yellow bellies. These mammals nest and live in small burrows. Their small bodies are compact and perfectly suited to burrowing.

Vultures

These creatures are nature's "cleanup" crews. They eat decayed roadkill. Their intestines are extremely tolerant. Vultures perch on live trees, but their droppings are so powerful that it kills bark and hence causes trees to become leafless and appear to be dead. Vultures have a wingspan of approximately six feet and weigh about six pounds. They typically spread their wings while perching. During flight, vultures soar for long periods then flap their wings quickly to maintain their altitude.

Black and turkey vultures

Turkey vultures can smell, whereas black vultures cannot. After a turkey vulture finds a carcass, black vultures immediately show up to join in the meal. Black vultures are capable of tearing meat off bones while turkey vultures cannot.

Whales

Whales are mammals who have no sweat glands because they live in the water and don't really need them. Spermaceti whale oil was a common fuel used in early oil lamps in lighthouses, and in homes as well.

I attended a lecture titled "The Changing Face of Whale Trauma: What We Know and Have to Do," given by Professor Michael Moore, MB, PhD—a veterinarian and senior scientist in the Biology Department—at the Woods Hole Oceanographic Institution (WHOI) in Woods Hole, Cape Cod, Massachusetts on December 9, 2022. I thought my readers would be interested in the following excerpt:

> Every thought, decision, and action each of us take, has implications for ourselves, all the other humans we impact knowingly or not, and the animals we study and endeavor to conserve and steward.

You can view the full lecture at https://www.mbl.edu/events/falmouth-forum/2021-22-falmouth-forum. I feel this excerpt is in support of my thoughts concept.

Blue whales

The blue whale is the largest animal on planet Earth! They are close to four hundred thousand pounds and approximately one hundred feet long. Their tongue alone weighs about 5,400 pounds or as much as an average elephant, and their heart is about the size of a VW Beetle! Blue whale babies are the largest in whale infants. A calf weighs about eight thousand pounds, and their height is around twenty-seven feet at birth.

Spermaceti oil is created in the spermaceti organ inside the whale's head. This organ may contain as much as five hundred gallon of spermaceti. Two theories for the spermaceti organ's biological function suggest it either controls buoyancy or acts as a focusing apparatus for the whale's sense of echolocation. Which animal preys most on other animals? The answer is the blue whale. They eat approximately forty million krill in a typical day of dining. Over a lifetime, the blue whale will eat one trillion krill; if you ate one krill per second, twenty-four hours a day, it would take thirty-two thousand years to match the appetite of the blue whale!

A blue whale's life span is identical to that of a human! Their gestation period is eleven months, and for the first eight months, an infant blue whale drinks enough milk each day to fill a fifty-five gallon drum! The young will grow at a rate of nine pounds per hour! The blue whale is the most prolific killer in the world. They are the biggest carnivore on the planet and the biggest creature to have ever lived in all of history.

White whale

Here are some interesting facts about white whales:

- The white whale is easily recognizable by their white coloring and roundish head.
- White whales are social animals and are one of the most vocal of all whales.
- Dives may last up to twenty-five minutes in depths of over two thousand feet.
- Born dark gray then turn completely white in about eight years.
- They are capable of swimming backward.
- They do not have a dorsal fin, but they do have a tough dorsal ridge.
- They have a thick layer of blubber to insulate them from icy arctic waters.

- The vertebrae in the neck are not fused together, allowing them move their head up, down, left, and right.
- Threats include climate change, hunting, oil spills, and pollution. Their predators are polar bears and killer whales.
- They are slow swimmers.

Wolverines

There are only less than 1,000 Wolverines left in the lower 48 states, with the largest population of Wolverines in Glacier Bay, Alaska. Wolverines are very social animals and can survive in the most difficult climates including mountain terrain and areas with subzero temperatures. They can prey on small as well as large animals such as moose.

Wolves

Wolves do not howl at the moon; they howl as a means of communicating with one another. Their howl can be heard for up to six miles. The wolf's life span can be up to thirteen years in the wild. Their average foot size is about four inches wide by about five inches long. Adult heights are up to three feet from the ground to the shoulders. Wolves weigh up to 180 pounds for males and up to 120 pounds for females. Adults can be up to five feet in length.

Wolves have over two hundred million scent cells. They can hear up to six miles away in a forest or about twenty times better than a human. Their jaw has a crushing power of about 1,500 pounds per square inch! They have forty-two teeth. The long muzzle of a wolf ends with a hypersensitive nose one hundred times better than the nose of a human. Wolves are the largest in the dog family.

Female wolves give birth in caves or holes in the ground called dens, which provide protection against weather and predators. A wolf's gestation period is between sixty-three and sixty-five days. Baby wolves, on average, are born in litters of four to six pups. The mother must massage her cub's belly with her tongue in order to stimulate urination.

Wolf pups weigh about a pound, and they cannot see or hear. Their color is blue at birth. At two weeks old, the pups open their eyes and learn to walk. They grow teeth then leave the den a week later. The eyes turn yellow between eight and sixteen weeks of age. Due to various diseases, malnutrition, and starvation, the mortality rate of wild wolf pups is approximately 30 to 60 percent.

Part 2
Cold-Blooded

Introduction

The internal temperatures of cold-blooded creatures automatically adjust to their environment and assume the temperature of their surroundings. Such creators are hot when their environment is hot, and they are cold when their environment is cold. Cold-blooded creatures are active in warmer environments and sluggish in colder environments. This is because their muscle activity depends on chemical reactions which respond quickly when it is hot and slowly when it is cold. Cold-blooded creatures can convert much more of their food into body mass compared to warm-blooded animals.

Since cold-blooded animals do not have to burn a lot of food to maintain a constant body temperature, they are more energy-efficient and can survive for longer periods without food. A cold-blooded animal cannot regulate its body temperature, so the level of activity highly depends upon the temperature of its surroundings. Therefore, they lie around in the sun to keep themselves warm as well as to increase their metabolism. Some cold-blooded animals shiver to stay warm when in cold environments. Snakes, lizards, toads, frogs, salamanders, and most turtles will hibernate during cool winters.

In addition to the cold-blooded animals discussed in this chapter, I have included several of our amazing insect species as well. Although it's impossible to know the total amount of different insect species on the planet, insect researchers (entomologists) believe there may be as many as twenty to thirty million! However, this number of insect species represent over 62 percent of all living creatures on Earth.

Advantages of being cold-blooded

Cold-blooded creatures use less energy to survive and, therefore, consumes much less food than warm-blooded animals. They can live in all areas, climates, and locations having less food available, such as in the deserts. It's more difficult for bacteria and viruses to live inside cold-blooded creatures because their body temperature frequently fluctuates. It's more difficult for insects to starve to death because they need only a fraction of the calories required by warm-blooded animals of relative size.

Disadvantages of being cold-blooded

Cold-blooded creatures need to be warm and active in order to find a mate and to reproduce. Cold-blooded animals can hardly move during cold weather making them easy prey. They have difficulty surviving in artic and extreme hot regions. They cannot remain active and seek food in a wide range of outdoor temperatures unless they can become warm enough to do so.

Alligators

The American alligators are located in swamps and marshlands from North Carolina to Central Texas, to South Florida usually in freshwater as they cannot tolerate salt water for long periods because they lack salt glands. Alligators can stay under water for several hours. However, they place their nostrils above water occasionally in order to breathe. Alligators can go for months without food. They never get sick, and they live for decades.

Lengths are typically sixteen feet; record is nineteen feet. Alligator stomachs are about the size of a football, and they can only eat small portions of their prey. They die in numbers whenever droughts last for several months. Their upper mouth is solid bone and extremely powerful. Their teeth do not protrude when their mouth is closed. Alligator mouths have a broad-rounded snout as opposed to those of crocodiles.

Ants and Termites

Researchers claim that ants are visible only when temperatures are above 58°F. Ants are the only creatures with the largest brain relative to its body size and can carry an object of their body weight. Why are ants so strong? It's a physics thing…smaller animals are relatively stronger, much like a smaller bubble is stronger than a larger bubble. Termites drag grass blades into their tunnels, then other termites mix the grass with soil to make compost. Termite queens give birth every fifteen seconds, or approximately thirty thousand a day.

Differences between ants and termites

Ants	Termites
Elbowed antennas (bent)	Straight antennas
Thin waist	Full waist
May have two wing sets of uneven lengths	Two wing sets of even lengths

Aphids

Aphids feed by piercing the tissue of a plant then sucking up the sap. However, much of what the aphid consumes goes to waste. The excess sugar is eliminated in the form of droplets. A single plant can have as many as thousands of aphids. Some aphids have tubular pipes on their hind ends like tiny tailpipes. These pipes serve as a defensive mechanism. When threatened, the aphid releases a waxy, sticky fluid substance which gums up the mouth of their predators. If all else fails, aphids drop and roll off their host plant to escape their predators. Because aphids survival depends on their numbers, they can reproduce without males. Aphids are born pregnant and give birth to live young. The aphid's eggs begin to develop as soon as ovulation occurs without any fertilization. Aphids live for only about three weeks.

Bees

Here are interesting facts about bees:

- The typical buzzing sound from bees is caused by their wings moving at over eleven thousand times per minute.
- Bees have two wings on each side of their bodies, which hook together to form one pair of wings while flying, then the wings unhook when they are standing still.
- About 90 percent of wild plants and about 75 percent of all crops depend on pollination.
- The average bee only makes about one teaspoon of honey during its lifetime.
- A single bee weighs about 0.00025 pounds or 0.004 ounces.
- It takes about 680 bees flying about thirty-three thousand miles to accumulate about six pounds of nectar from about one million flowers in order to make about ten ounces of honey.
- Bees can fly up to twenty miles per hour for about six miles.
- In warm weather, bees collect water and line up in a circle around the hive entrance. Using their wings, the bees fan the water so that it evaporates into the air. They then fan the cool air so that it circulates around the hive as a sort of central air conditioning.
- During cold weather, bees keep their hives warm by swarming together to generate body heat.
- Queen bees leave their hives once in their lifetime in order to mate.
- Bees are meticulous creatures. They groom each other and keep their hives incredibly clean.
- Bees make large round wax cell nests above as well as below the ground.
- The hexagonal shape of the bee honeycomb is the most efficient design. This pattern allows for each cell to be packed without any empty spaces in between the cells.

- Bees steal honey from other beehives. If such a robber makes it into another hive unnoticed, they will acquire the scent of the hive then can repeatedly return without being detected as an outside intruder.
- Honey and pollen are the main bee's diet. The queen's diet, however, must be richer in honey, which gives her protein and carbohydrates needed for fertility.
- Bees have six legs and five eyes, two large compound eyes on either side of its head, and three simple eyes which distinguish light from dark.
- The queen bee can lay as many as two thousand eggs per day.
- Bees are social creatures and not aggressive. However, they will sting but only to protect their hives or when provoked.
- Being stung by a bee means that you have been injected with melittin, which is a venom that causes pain and a number of other symptoms, including a raised red area around the sting.
- There are over twenty-thousand species of bees in the world, four thousand are native to the United States.
- There are more than one hundred bees in each colony.
- Only female bees possess stingers. Females die after the first sting because the barbs on their stinger prevents the stinger from being retracted and, therefore, the stinger gets ripped away from their bodies.
- Bees have more hair than hornets or wasps.
- They are vegetarians but feed nectar to their young.
- Most bee colors are typically orange, brown, or green and blue. However, some bees are yellow or black.
- Bees are not found in Antarctica.
- Bees are not wasps, yellow jackets, or hornets because bees only pollinate and do not prey on other insects.
- Bees have a brain about the size of a poppy seed.
- They have the ability to use their footprints to distinguish among their own scent, the scent of relatives, or the scent

of strangers. Thus they can avoid landing on flowers that have already been visited.

- A study revealed that bees cannot fly at night or in the darkness. Bees flying in a lighted room immediately fell to the floor as soon as the lights were turned off. However, some bees in the tropics have adapted themselves to fly in the darkness.

Various names of bees

Social bees, solitary bees, bumblebees, mason bees, carpenter bees, sweat bees, leaf-cutter bees, cuckoo bees, orchid bees, and nocturnal bees.

Help a bee

If you come across a bee that appears to be struggling, it may be that it is simply resting. However, if you believe the bee is in trouble, the best thing you can do is gently put the bee onto a flower. If there are no flowers around, then mix fifty-fifty white sugar and water to give the bee carbohydrates it needs to fly. Simply place a drop or two up to the front end of the bee in a sheltered place and allow the bee time to recuperate. Do not offer honey or brown sugar as it's harder for bees to digest. We can all do our part to help a bee. We can also inform friends about making their outside spaces bee-friendly. Plant rows of flowers in the garden so bees have plenty of access to nectar.

After giving a tour of the Nobska Lighthouse on a hot and humid afternoon, I was walking along the pathway back to my car when I spotted a struggling honeybee on the walkway. I carefully picked the honeybee up as a young couple were watching and asking what I was doing. I explained I was looking for some flowers to place the honeybee as it needed nectar to build up its strength. Of course, there were following questions. I placed the honeybee on a leaf by a flower and left it there. Did it survive? I don't know, but it was the best thing to do at that moment; otherwise, it would not have survived on the pathway. Yes, I felt good about what I did, and I had many positive thoughts about how precious and vital these creatures are for our existence.

Dinner for the queen

If a queen bee dies in her hive, the bee workers can create a new queen bee by selecting an unhatched bee and feed it a type of food which will cause it to develop into a fertile queen.

Removing a stinger

Removing a stinger is important because the longer the stinger is inside your skin, the more venom it will release into your body. There are several ways to remove a bee stinger. If you wish to use tweezers, you may need to use a needle to first dig away surrounding area of the skin before tweezers can effectively be used to pull a stinger out. You can also quickly remove a stinger by using your fingernails to scrape the bee stinger out and away from your skin. This will limit the amount of injected melittin.

Temperature

During colder weather, bees raise their internal body temperature above the temperature of their environment by rapidly moving their wings to generate body heat. Bees are not only pollinators of flowering plants, fruits, and vegetables, but they are also parasites of other arthropods, including pest insects. These parasites limit the population growth of the insect, which would otherwise destroy most types of crops.

Reproduction

Queen bees are the only members of the colony that are able to survive the winter. In April or May, each queen selects a suitable location, constructs a small nest, and begins raising sterile daughter workers. These workers take over the duties of enlarging and maintaining the nest, searching for food, and caring for the offspring while the queen bee functions only to produce more eggs.

The queen bee lays all her eggs within the colony. The queen bee fertilizes each egg as it is being laid using stored sperm. The queen occasionally will not fertilize an egg so that these eggs will have only half as many genes as the queen bee or the workers to, therefore, develop into male drones.

Carpenter bees

Carpenter bees are not social insects, and they live for only one year. This bee is a large insect with a hairy yellow thorax, a shiny black abdomen, and resembles female bumblebees. In the spring, they bore in wood and make a long tunnel to lay their eggs and to store their pollen. New females reuse old tunnels year after year. Carpenter bees drill into wood or into the face of wooden members then turn and tunnel with the grain. Males have no stingers but attack intruders. Since these bees are not social, there is no worker caste to protect their nest. Stings from females are rare. New adults emerge after the middle of summer and can be seen feeding on flowers.

Honeybees

More books are written about honeybees than any other types of insects. They live in trees or human structures in groups of over forty thousand. They produce and store honey in their nests, which they build from their own natural wax. Honeybees produce wax combs which consist of many hexagonal cells that have walls about two thousandths of an inch thick but strong enough to support twenty-five times their own weight. Honeybee wings flap over eleven thousand times per minute, thus making their distinctive buzz.

This guy looks busy
(Photo by the author)

They are highly social insects and communicate with each other on the directions and distances to nectar and pollen. They make combs of waxen cells placed side by side that provide spaces to raise their young and to store honey. The bee colony lives on the stored honey throughout winters, and therefore, it's the reason a colony can exist for years. Honeybees stay warm by crowding themselves together and flapping their wings rapidly to generate body heat. When colony populations are too high, the queen bee will often move part of the colony to a different location. Bees swarm together to find hollow trees to start their new colonies. They occasionally work their way into open spaces in building walls as well. Over one third of our food was pollinated by bees, and most are from honeybees. Honeybees harvest nectar from flowers and pollen for carbohydrates and protein.

Honeybee drones. Honeybee drones are male bees and have no stingers. Drones do not collect food or pollen from flowers. Instead, their sole purpose is to mate with the queen bee. Should the colony become low on food supply, drones are often chased out of their hives.

Honeybee workers. Undeveloped female honeybees are the workers and are the smallest bees in the colony. A colony can have up to sixty thousand workers. The life span of a worker bee depends upon the time of year. Her life expectancy can be as long as thirty-five days. Workers feed the queen bee and the larvae. They guard the hive entrance, and they help to keep their hives cool by rapidly fanning their wings. They also collect nectar to make the honey.

Pest management for honeybees. A honeybee colony inside a house wall can cause major problems. The bees can chew through the walls and fly inside any room. Their storage of large amounts of honey would then invite other bees and wasps. Their dead bees shredded larval skins, wax caps from combs, and other materials will attract other insects, such as beetles and moths. When a bee colony is found in a building wall, it must be immediately removed.

After honeybees move their colonies to a different location and the nest becomes vacant, the vacant nest may then be safely removed. The entrance hole should be caulked or repaired. If the nest is not removed, the wax combs will melt and allow honey to flow down inside the walls. Honey stain cannot be removed; the walls will have to be replaced, otherwise the honey will attract bees and wasps. The comb wax will also attract wax moths that may remain for several years.

Butterflies

Butterflies taste with their hind feet and can see colors of red, green, and yellow. The average butterfly can fly up to speeds of twelve miles per hour. Butterflies have skeletons on the outside of their bodies, and their hearts are in their thorax. They have a brain and can remember what they learned as caterpillars.

Only a handful of purple butterflies exist around the world. Although butterflies do not feel pain, they will not attempt to fly in the rain because the raindrops could do major damage to their delicate wings. Typically, the life span of a butterfly can be up to a month. Butterflies cannot fly if their body temperature is less than

86°F. However, some species of butterflies have adapted to fly in temperatures as low as the mid-60°F.

Dead leaf butterfly

I have never seen a dead leaf butterfly until one landed on one of the Adirondack chairs on my deck. Joanne was quick to identify the insect as a dead leaf butterfly. I quickly took a photo for fear that it would soon fly away, then I did some research. The dead leaf butterfly has an interesting way to protect itself from predators. With many dead leaves scattered around its habitat, the dead leaf butterfly has plenty of places to hide.

Their wings are colored on the top, making this display easy for birds to spot when flying. Not a strong or fast flier and doesn't fly much, but when they do they fly back and forth in an erratic pattern, they prevent birds from predicting or tracking their movements and thereby making them more difficult to catch. However, when at rest and its wings are closed, it's a much different story. The way in which their wings fold up, the light brown coloring and the raised veins all resemble a dead leaf.

Dead leaf butterfly
(Photo by the author)

When the dead leaf butterfly finds food, it settles down and doesn't move unless threatened or when it's time to search for more food. With a forest floor covered in dead leaves, this butterfly can simply sink to the bottom and close its wings for camouflage. Even hanging upside down from a branch, it looks like a dead leaf rather than a butterfly. It often stays on the forest floor and waits for fallen fruit. This insect also feeds on sticky sap flowing from trees.

Monarch butterflies

Male monarch butterflies have a black "scent spot" on one of the veins located on each of the hind wings while females do not. Monarchs can live up to five weeks. Female monarch butterflies may lay several hundred eggs during her lifetime. Eggs hatch after about four to six days during average spring and summer temperatures. Monarch butterflies migrate over two thousand miles as they fly to Central Mexico every fall and can fly over one thousand miles without stopping.

I vividly recall an event, which took place during one of my many dinghy trips from the dock on the mainland of Norwalk, Connecticut, to our moored *Catalina 30* off Sprite Island. The trip was only about a mile long. Soon after underway, I noticed a monarch butterfly flying along the side of my dinghy and headed in the same direction. To me, he (or she) seemed desperate to make land as it was flying somewhat erratically. Without knowing anything about these beautiful creatures, I began to talk to him in my attempt to encourage him to "hop aboard" for a free ride. Otherwise, I really didn't think he would make it. Although I knew this was a challenge, I continued talking nonstop as I had a full half mile to go, and I was getting more and more concerned for his life.

When I finally reached my mooring after what seemed like an hour, I figured the monarch would either land to rest on my sailboat or perhaps rest at nearby Sprite Island, but instead, he continued flying until he was out of sight! I later did some research and learned that it was estimated that as colder weather approaches in the fall, millions of butterflies leave their homes in the United States to fly incredible distance of several thousands of miles to Mexico then return to the United States again in the following spring. Only about 4 percent of the world's butterflies are located in the United States.

Painted lady butterflies

Painted lady butterflies migrate from Africa to England and travel over three thousand miles to accomplish this voyage. The painted lady is one of the most familiar butterflies in the world found on nearly every continent and climates except Australia and Antarctica. They are a favorite subject of study in school classrooms and are a familiar visitor to gardens.

Painted lady butterflies have some interesting attributes.

- Thistle plants are painted lady's favorite nectar plant.
- The painted lady migrates independently of any seasonal or geographic patterns. In the spring, they fly only several feet above the ground, making them highly vulnerable to colliding with vehicles. During other times, they migrate at higher altitudes, showing up unexpectedly in various areas.
- Painted lady butterflies are capable of speeds up to thirty miles per hour, accounting for why they arrive in areas well before their migrating cousins.
- Crop damage occurs during the larval stages when caterpillars eat foliage after hatching from eggs.
- Males patrol their territory for receptive females then fly to a treetop to mate overnight.
- Unlike other caterpillars, painted lady build their silk tents on various plants.
- Painted lady typically congregate in small plant areas on overcast days. However, on sunny days, they head for open areas filled with colorful flowers.

Chameleons

Chameleons are part of the lizard family and have the ability to change color as a means of camouflage. Their behavior reveals their intentions to other chameleons. Chameleon eyelids are fused and cover the entire eyeball, except for a small hole to see through; each of their two eyes may be moved independently to have a full 360-degree vision. The chameleon preys on insects, mice, and many small creatures. They capture prey by thrusting their tongue out at high speeds and can see an insect five about ten feet away. They are also capable of seeing ultraviolet light.

Crickets

In warm weather, the outside temperature can be estimated by the amount of cricket chirps heard. Count the number of chirps within a fifteen-second period then add thirty-seven to get the outside temperature in Fahrenheit.

Crocodiles

They are typically called the American crocodile. Its length is approximately twelve feet; record is fifteen feet in the US and twenty-three feet in South America. Crocodiles have a long, tapering, pointed snout with conspicuous display of teeth while the mouth is closed. This feature distinguishes crocodiles from alligators. Colors of crocodiles range from tannish gray to greenish gray. The American crocodile lives in salt water, ponds, and swamps. They are located along the southern coastline of Florida, the Florida Keys, Mexico, Central America, South America, Colombia, Venezuela, Ecuador, Peru, the Caribbean islands, Cayman, Jamaica, Hispaniola, Martinique, and Margarita.

Their diet consists of crabs, turtles, fish, snakes, birds, small mammals, dogs, insects, and spiders. Mating generally occurs during late winter to early spring. Females lay hard-shelled eggs around April or May then typically buries her eggs in a hole, a pile of dirt, or on a beach. After the eggs hatch, she will transport her young to the water using her mouth.

Damselfly

Eyes of the damselfly are large, spherical, and protrude from the sides of their head. The thorax (the area where the wings are attached to their body) is about the same width as their abdomen. The forewings and hind wings are similar in size and shape, usually smaller compared to those of dragonflies. Resting at a pond, its wing would look different from dragonfly wings. Rather than holding its wings flat and to the sides of its body, damselflies hold their wings straight up, pressed together over the top of their thorax. If wings are lying flat, parallel to the ground, you are looking at a dragonfly. If the wings are held over its back and pressed together, you are looking at a damselfly.

Dragonfly

Dragonflies spend their first year in water as nymphs and eat mosquito larvae, small fish, aquatic insects, worms, and small tadpoles. After they surface, they dry out and live for another five months. While on the fly, they consume mosquitoes, flies, ants, termites, butterflies, gnats, bees, and other insects. They tend to hunt in groups whenever large colonies of ants or termites are present.

Dragonflies have two eyes, each with thirty thousand smaller eyes. Their eyes are broadly rounded and lie mostly flat against their head. They have legs, but they cannot walk. They can fly in six different directions: forward, backward, left, right, up, and down. How incredible! The thorax is broader than the abdomen. Forewings and hind wings are different shapes. A dragonfly can eat food equal to its own weight in about thirty minutes.

Although dragonflies have the ability and equipment to bite humans, they will not bite unless you handle them roughly, then they can give you a painful experience. They have very powerful jaws, which they use for chewing up other flying insects. Many species of dragonflies are brightly colored mostly for communication among other dragonflies. Females have protruding body parts at the tip of the abdomen that resemble a stinger, but they are actually a device used to deposit eggs below the surface of the water.

A bit unusual, but dragonflies have been known to land on your shoulder, wait for mosquitoes to fly by, leave your shoulder to catch the pest, then return to chew and dine right on your shoulder.

Longest migration

As reported, the tiny dragonfly (1.5 inches) migrates annually about ten thousand miles round trip at an altitude of about three thousand feet while the previous record held by the monarch butterfly migrates annually about five thousand miles round trip.

Fish

Fish can't see in the dark, but they can find food when there is no light because of the vibrations that food makes. All fish are very sensitive to vibrations. They have a lateral line organ (LLO) running along its skin from its gills to its tail. All along the lateral line organ are openings in the fish's skin. These openings allow water vibrations to reach sensory organs, which are located under the lateral line.

Fish who live in areas where there are cold winters move to deeper waters during the colder months or migrate to warmer waters. Some fish have a special protein in their blood which acts like antifreeze to help them survive in very cold water temperatures.

Lobsters

There are two kinds of lobsters in United States waters: the "true" American lobster and the spiny lobster. Female lobsters can carry live sperm for up to two years, but by law, if a female lobster carrying eggs is caught, she must be put back into the water. No one has yet found a way to determine the exact age of a lobster. Lobster babies swim at the water surface for twenty-five days but only about 1 percent survive.

A freshly laid lobster egg is about 1/16 of an inch. A female lobster may carry approximately eight thousand eggs for nine to twelve months, and then for another nine to twelve months attached under her tail. When the eggs hatch, the larvae will float near the surface for four to six weeks. The few that survive will settle to the bottom and continue to develop as baby lobsters. From every fifty thousand eggs, only two lobsters are expected to survive to legal size.

Can lobsters feel pain when boiled? Seafood sellers may tell you differently, but lobsters do feel pain, and they suffer immensely when they are broiled alive. Most scientists agree that a lobster's nervous system is quite sophisticated. A lobster's brain is located in its throat, its nervous system in its abdomen, its teeth in its stomach, and its kidneys in its head. It also hears using its legs, tastes with its feet, and tends to favor one front claw, which could mean they could be right- or left-clawed.

Here are some interesting facts about lobsters:

- The true (American) lobster has claws on its front four legs whereby the spiny lobster does not have claws.
- Spiny lobsters have a pair of horns above its eyes, whereby the true lobster does not. Spiny lobsters have long spiny antennas and are found in warm waters. Lobster tails on a menu are usually from spiny lobsters.
- The record weight for the American lobster is forty-five pounds.
- Inshore lobsters tend to stay in one place, seldom moving more than a mile or so. The record travel is 225 miles covered by a lobster tagged off the continental shelf and recovered at Port Jefferson, Long Island, New York. Lobster blood is colorless. However, when exposed to oxygen, the blood develops a bluish color.
- The American lobster is also known as the Massachusetts lobster, the Maine lobster, the Canadian lobster, or the North Atlantic lobster.

- The American lobster is found on the East Coast of North America from Newfoundland to North Carolina. Approximately 80 percent of US lobsters come from Massachusetts, Rhode Island, and Maine.
- Lobsters usually hunt for food at night and mainly catch fresh food, such as fish, crabs, clams, mussels, sea urchins, and sometimes even other lobsters!
- Conservation measures include safeguarding lobsters smaller than 3 1/4 inches measured from the rear of the eye socket to the rear of the main body shell. Lobsters smaller, or egg-bearing females, must be returned to the sea unharmed.
- Lobster traps must have escape vents to allow illegal size lobsters to exit the trap.
- Lobsters less than 1 1/2 inches hide in seaweeds and rocky places.
- Lobsters 1 1/2 to 3 1/2 inches live in coastal and offshore areas.
- The lobster is a gill breather, and moisture is essential for survival.
- Fresh water is lethal to a lobster. They have salty blood and tissues, which require seawater for survival.
- Lobster's liver turns green when cooked and is considered a delicacy.
- Lobsters spoil rapidly after death, which is why many buyers insist on receiving them alive.
- Lobsters come in many different colors except red. However, all lobsters turn red when boiled.
- Lobsters have the ability to regrow some of their body parts, such as the claws, walking legs, and antennas, which suggests they have a low sensitivity to pain.
- The lobster's stomach is located close to their mouth, and the food they consume is actually chewed in the stomach between three grinding surfaces.

- Lobsters smell their food by using four small antennas on the front of their heads and tiny sensing hairs that cover their bodies. Their sense of smell is excellent.
- The Massachusetts Lobstermen's Association claimed a record when they caught Big George in 1974 off Cape Cod. The lobster weighed 37.4 pounds with a length of 2.1 feet.

Oysters

Oysters have the ability to change sex from male to female and vice versa! Females can produce up to one hundred million eggs annually. Their shells are semitranslucent and used to make decorative objects. Pearl oysters are capable to secrete pearls. However, such pearls are typically of no value. Researchers have not determined if oysters have a brain. The most common predators of oysters are humans, crabs, seabirds, and starfish.

Sharks

Typically, sharks swim only about one to two miles daily to conserve energy needed for chasing their prey. Because of conserving their energy, they are capable of amazing fast bursts of speed while catching prey. Sharks only eat about every thirty to sixty days after consuming big prey, such as seals, porpoises, or dolphins.

Shark ecology

Some species can change their body temperature to go deeper into the water. Their sensory organs are located on their nose and capable of detecting electrical currents through the water.

Great white sharks

The great white shark can only survive in salt water. They are about fifteen feet long and can swim at speeds of about thirty-five miles per hour. They have five rows of teeth, and any tooth that is lost gets replaced. The great white shark can smell blood up to about three miles away. They can leap about ten feet above the surface of the water, and they typically live to about seventy years of age.

Bull sharks

The name "bull shark" comes from their snout and head-butting their prey before killing them. Bull sharks can survive in salt or fresh water. The fastest speed they can swim is about twenty-five miles per hour. Their diet consists of smaller sharks, stingrays, dolphins, other bull sharks, birds, sea turtles, and crustaceans. They also have the worst bite in all shark species as their teeth have a bite force of about 1/2 ton at the back of the mouth and about 1/4 ton at the front.

Basking sharks

Most of us think basking sharks don't have teeth. They do, but their teeth are only the size of rice grains.

Gnats

Gnats are very tiny flying insect. They can be both biting and nonbiting. They typically fly in large numbers called clouds. They are no bigger than a few grains of salt and are attracted to the fluids secreted from human and animal eyes. Adult gnats have antennas and are generally slender bodied with long and narrow wings. Some gnats are so tiny they are barely visible. They are bloodsucking flies commonly known as biting gnats, sand flies among other names. In general, gnats go through the four life stages of egg, larva, pupa, and adult, similar to other flies.

Fungus gnats

The fungus gnat lay their eggs in moist organic debris or soil, which hatch into larvae. The larvae feed on organic matter, such as leaf mold, mulch, compost, grass clippings, and fungi; then adults eventually emerge from the pupae. At a temperature of 75°F, the cycle takes approximately seventeen days: three days as eggs, ten days as larvae, and four days as pupae. Warmer temperatures allow more rapid development.

Other gnats begin their lives as eggs laid in water or on aquatic plants. The aquatic larvae dwell in ponds, pools, stale water-filled containers, clogged rain gutters, or wet soil. They generally feed on plant matter. Adults live only long enough to reproduce, and they may form large mating swarms, often around dusk. The life cycle generally takes four to five weeks. Adult nonbiting gnats do not damage plants but nevertheless considered a nuisance.

To prevent gnats from spreading, eliminate their favorable living conditions by reducing excess moisture, drain pools of standing water, and remove decaying organic matter. To control gnats in the home, pressurized aerosol sprays are effective. Other control measures in the household include turning off unnecessary lights at dusk and sealing vents and other openings.

Horseshoe Crabs

Horseshoe crabs predate dinosaurs! The oldest known horseshoe crab was estimated to be about 450 million years old and thus why they are often referred to as "living fossils." Their primary sets of legs are used to move about. However, since horseshoe crabs have no jaws, they use another pair of legs called pincers to crunch their food before placing into their mouth, which is located at the base of the pincers. Horseshoe crabs eat worms, algae, clams, and other small prey that they root out in the sediment on the ocean floor.

Horseshoe crabs are not dangerous. Their tails aren't poisonous or venomous, but instead, their tail is used to navigate through water and to flip themselves over whenever they get stuck upside down. Flap-like gills near their abdomen enable horseshoe crabs to breathe underwater and also used to swim upside down.

During high tide in the spring, horseshoe crabs mate and lay their eggs at night by the shoreline. Females deposit around four thousand eggs in clusters up to about twenty thousand eggs during a single night. It takes two to four weeks for horseshoe crab eggs to hatch although most of their eggs will not survive to adulthood. Tiny crabs emerge and find shallow, sheltered waters to live in. They shed their old shells several times in the first year. Their shells darken as they age. They reach maturity at about ten years of age.

With a total of nine eyes, along with various light receptors near their tail, these creatures have superexcellent vision. Their two compound eyes are used to locate potential mates while their smaller eyes are sensitive to ultraviolet light. The remaining eyes are used to detect nearby movement.

Horseshoe crabs have a protein containing copper rather than iron, which gives their blood its bright blue color. They do not have white blood cells like humans have, which fight off infection. Instead, they have cells that attack the bad cells by trapping them in a wall of "goo." Johns Hopkins discovered that horseshoe crab blood cells can be used to test the safety of vaccines and other drugs before approval. The shell produces a chemical which keeps it looking smooth. Nothing can grow on its shell. Medical research is using this chemical in developing medical products. Bandages were developed for burn patients, for example, to prevent infections and to allow bandages to remain on longer instead of having to remove them from burned skin. Medical research is also using the blood from horseshoe crabs to heal patients.

Shorebirds rely on the fat and protein-packed horseshoe crab eggs for their long migration of about nine thousand miles from South America to the Arctic. Fishermen use horseshoe crabs as bait, causing their population to become smaller. However, in some states, this activity is illegal.

Insects

Insects belong to the bug family, and most have mouthparts adapted for piercing and sucking. They also have two pairs of wings, such as the common stink bugs and bedbugs. Insects are arthropods (a type of invertebrate animal that lack a backbone). Their small size and ability to fly helps them to escape from predators and travel to new environments. Since they are so small, they need only small amounts of food and can live in very small cracks and spaces. Insects are an extremely diverse type of cold-blooded creatures. The rate at which they grow and develop depend mainly on the temperature of their environment.

Characteristics of insects

Insects pass through four stages of life—(1) egg, (2) larva (or nymph), (3) pupa, and (4) adult—and generally have four characteristics in common:

- Three body parts (head, thorax, and abdomen)
- Six jointed legs
- Two antennas to sense the environment
- Exoskeleton (outside skeleton)

Assassin bugs

Some insects possess half wings, such as the box elder bugs, milkweed bugs, assassin bugs, and stink bugs. True bugs have stylet (mouths like a straw) that are used to suck out juices from plants. The assassin bugs use their stylets to suck blood from other insects. Their forewings also have thick bases and membranous tips. The hind wings are usually clear and tucked underneath the front wings. The assassin bug is excellent for gardens as they prey on caterpillars and grasshoppers. Adults tend not to fly.

Where are insects found?

We cannot travel anywhere on land and not find insects. They can even be found in the frozen extremes of the Artic and Antarctica. Insects are in the soil under our feet, in the air above our head, plants, and animals around us. The only place where insects are not commonly found is in the oceans. Insects eat more plants than all other creatures on Earth combined. Without insects, we would have a world covered with dead plants and animals. In addition to all this, insects are a major food source for a wide range of animal species.

Jellyfish

Jellyfish are not considered fish. A fascinating fact about jellyfish is that they don't have brains, a heart, blood, or any bones. Some jellyfish have ways of detecting obstacles that can be compared to sight, but they don't have real eyes. It is a mystery how they can process the information from their "sight" since they don't have brains. They react directly on food and danger via nerve impulses without having any brain to process the impulses. A sting from a jellyfish can be extremely painful. A hot water treatment may be the best remedy.

The world's largest known jellyfish has a diameter approximately eight feet. Their tentacles can grow to be half the length of a football field. Jellyfish use jet propulsion to make their way through the oceans. Some jellyfish are avid swimmers while others mostly drift with the currents. A species of jellyfish, the box jellyfish, or sea wasp kills more people each year than any other marine creature.

Box jellyfish

Box jellyfish have four different types of eyes on their dome-shaped body that detect light levels, color, and size of objects. One eye is located on the top of their body and the other on the bottom. Another set of eyes keeps the box jellyfish from running into obstacles as they swim along the ocean floor while making 180-degree turns around objects.

Ladybugs

Ladybugs can bite but only if they are threatened or mishandled. Male ladybugs are smaller than females, and it's very difficult to distinguish the difference. Females lay hundreds of eggs at a time. For defense, ladybugs fold in their legs, leaving only their hard shell exposed against predators, such as ants. Ladybugs fatten up for the winter by eating plenty of aphids and pollen then spend the winter in a state of suspended animation. They hide in buildings or under logs, rocks, or piles of leaves.

Mosquitoes

Male mosquitoes do not bite. Only female mosquitoes can bite people and animals to get a blood meal to produce their eggs. When a female mosquito bites, it pierces the skin using a special mouthpart to suck up blood. As the mosquito feeds, it injects saliva into the skin. The body reacts to the saliva, resulting in a bump and itching. Some people have only a mild reaction to a bite or bites while others react more severely. A large area of swelling, soreness, and redness may develop.

Here are some interesting facts about mosquitoes:

- Carbon dioxide gives mosquitoes the signal that blood is nearby, and since we exhale CO_2, we make it easy for these pests to locate us.
- Mosquitoes have six legs as do most insects.
- Mosquitoes have brains. Although very small, this organ is able to allow mosquitoes to see, move, taste, as well as detect cold and warm temperatures.
- Mosquitoes do defecate. Their waste can be either semi-solid or in liquid form.
- There are at least 2,700 known mosquito species in the world. Fortunately, there are only about 176 species in the United States.
- Mosquitoes are the deadliest creatures on the planet. They can carry dangerous diseases. More deaths have been reported as a result of mosquito bites than any other creature.
- Although mosquitoes don't have teeth, they bite with their mouthparts.
- Do mosquito bites hurt? Bites from mosquitoes are annoying and very itchy. Some people, however, experience pain but seldom during the process of biting.
- Mosquitoes cannot give or spread Lyme disease.

Moths

Hawk moth

This is an insect which can raise its body temperature well above the temperature of its surroundings when it is flying because of its huge wing muscles, which generate heat when in use.

Praying Mantis

The praying mantis is the only insect that can turn its head 360 degrees. They are one of my favorite insects because of the unique way they look and because their main diet consists of mosquitos and other biting insects.

Reptiles

Reptiles will lie perpendicular to the direction of the sun, thus maximizing the amount of sun rays falling on their skin. They will also expand their rib cage to increase their surface area and will darken their skin to absorb more heat. However, when a reptile is too hot, it will lie parallel to the sun's rays, thus minimizing exposure to the sun, go into a shady area, open its mouth wide, lighten its skin color, or burrow into cool soil. A reptile's immune system is more efficient when it is warmer. Since bacteria grows more slowly in lower temperatures, reptile body temperatures will lower when they develop an infection.

Snakes

Like most animals, snakes will defend themselves if threatened, injured, or captured. Even then, the defensive maneuvers of several species are nothing more offensive than releasing foul-smelling anal secretions. Other species attempt to frighten or intimidate potential enemies through bluff by flattening their heads, puffing up their bodies, rattling their tails, or hissing. In self-defense, some snakes will indeed bite, but except in cases of extremely rare venomous species, the resulting wounds are superficial. Many nonvenomous snakes possess short, thin, very sharp teeth that leave clean, shallow wounds (rarely requiring even a bandage), which carry no threat of disease. The important thing to remember is that unless you attempt to harm or capture a snake, it is almost impossible to get bitten.

Reproduction

Depending on the species, snakes may be egg layers or give birth to live young. They generally mate in the spring shortly after leaving whatever hollow, burrow, or rock crevice has sheltered them through winter hibernation. Egg layers usually deposit groups of eggs in dirt, beneath stones or logs, or in piles of decaying wood or vegetation during late spring or early summer. Most snakes hatch or born in late summer. Snakes do not take any responsibility for the care and protection of their young. They are on their own from birth. Most snakes mature at one or two years of age and may live up to twenty years in the wild.

Habitat

During the active season, snakes are rarely cold and are excellent at regulating their temperatures through behavior. Snakes occupy a wide range of habitats, including fields, forests, wetlands, ponds, lakes, streams, rocky hillsides, farmland, vacant lots, and residential neighborhoods. Within those habitats, snakes may travel along the ground, swim, climb trees and bushes, and venture below ground. Although some snakes do burrow, most snake holes are originally produced by chipmunks, mice, and other small mammals. However, many snakes utilize these burrows to hunt for food, shelter, and egg-laying sites.

Snakes can warm themselves by lying in the sun, lying on or under rocks, lumber stored in the sunlight, or by lying on pavement that hold the heat after dark. When the air temperature is too hot, they seek shelter in small mammal burrows, under rocks, or inside cool basements and cellars.

The food chain

Snakes are important to our ecosystem. All snakes are predators, and like many other creatures, they affect the balance of nature as both predators and prey. Depending on size and species, they feed on slugs, worms, insects, fish, other snakes, birds, bird eggs, and small mammals. Species such as the milk snake and the black rat snake consume large numbers of rodents. Their presence around barns is welcome by farmers, in particular the milk snake, because it regularly enters burrows and consume young mice and rats right in their nests. Garter, redbelly, and brown snakes frequently consume garden pests, such as slugs and certain soft-bodied insects.

Snakes find their prey by sight and scent and sometimes temperature, except for burrowing species. Snakes have excellent short-range vision, and their sense of smell is exceptional due to their harmless constantly flicking forked tongue that carries scent particles to a sensory organ on the roof of their mouth. Some species of snakes catch their prey by hunting them down or by ambush.

Some species kill their prey through venomous bites, by constriction, or by simply overpowering then swallowing their prey. Lacking chewing teeth, all snakes swallow their meals whole. Snakes may eat as often as several times a day or as seldom as once a month. Snakes and their eggs are often eaten by fish, other snakes, birds, skunks, raccoons, and possums. Birds are the snake's most feared predators. Songbirds consume great numbers of small snakes.

Hognose snake

An encounter with a hognose snake is an experience one may never forget. This great pretender puts on such a display when its alarmed that it actually looks and sounds far more dangerous than venomous snakes! He will inflate his body, hiss loudly, lunge about ferociously, and spread a cobra-type head. Despite this impressive display, he seldom bites.

If his bluff fails to drive off predators, the hognose will squirm about, vomit, roll on its back, let its tongue fall out, and displays the appearance of a dead snake. If turned upright, he will immediately roll on his back again. When danger is over, the hognose will turn upright, and be on his way.

Venomous snakes

The chances of receiving a bite from a venomous snake are low since these species of snakes are shy and try to avoid people. They will bite in self-defense. The strength of their venom is highly exaggerated.

Identification

Snakes around homes are quite harmless and nonvenomous. It is simple to recognize common snakes through use of a snake-identification guide. When we put a name and motivation to something, it tends to lose its ability to frighten us.

Spiders

The word "spider" comes from the German word "spinner" because spiders spin or weave silk. Spiders generate four types of silks of various strengths. Two spider strands of silk can stop a bat flying at approximately 40 MPH. Although spider silk is very strong, it is very difficult to accumulate in volumes to be of any use to us. Spiders cannot spin webs on chestnut wood, and this is why many homes in Europe are built using chestnut wood ceiling beams. A typical forty-foot high ceiling would otherwise be very difficult to clean!

Habits

Spiders cannot chew their food. When a bug is caught in their web, they bite it and inject venom, which either paralyzes or kills the bug. The bug's insides then turn into a liquid. The spider may drink the liquid or wrap it in silk to snack later. Spiders may have six, eight, or fewer eyes in front, but they mainly rely on touch and vibrations through their feet to navigate and find their prey. The retina of each eye can remain locked on their prey, then while they approach closer, they use their front-side eyes to judge distance to their prey. When their prey is less than an inch away, they leap. The spider senses movement of distant prey with their wide-angle side eyes then lock onto the moving prey with the large front-middle eyes, which provide a clear and focused telephoto image. Spiders do not eat plants but only other living insects. They eat more insects than birds do. If you stay more than a foot away from a spider, it cannot see you. Most spiders typically live for one to two years, but tarantulas can live up to six or twenty years.

Wolf spiders

These spiders have good vision and can hunt in dimmer light of dusk and moonlight. Their four large eyes help them spot prey movements in low light conditions. At night, wolf spiders can easily be spotted because their large eyes shine brightly. Wolf spiders chase and pounce on their prey.

Net-casting spiders

These spiders also have good vision with their eight eyes. The two in the rear are enormously large and provide low light night vision. Their curved compound lenses face forward like double headlights. Light-sensitive membranes are manufactured at night but vanish at dawn. This amazing arrangement enables these spiders to accurately track and "net" their prey at night.

Jumping spiders

These spiders have good vision and are very active during the day. Jumping spiders propel by their back legs and can jump greater than twenty times their body length. When hunting, their eyes see in three different directions by using three different sets of eyes.

Spider mites

Spider mites closely resemble spiders. They are very tiny and difficult to see with the naked eye. They suck out sap from pine trees using their mouthparts. The needles may turn brown then fall off.

Spider mites
(Photo courtesy of the US Department of Agriculture)

Predators of mites include ladybugs, beetles, and other similar insects. Since insecticides kills beneficial predators as well as mites, they should not be used unless absolutely necessary; otherwise using them may cause the death of natural predators of the mite. Mites may be removed with a strong water spray applied regularly.

Turtles

Turtles are air-breathing reptiles and are some of the most amazing sea creatures. With their unique shells, these creatures stand out among other sea and land reptiles. There are about 360 species of turtles in the world. Popular species include hawksbill turtles, leatherback turtles, flatback turtles, loggerheads, red-eared sliders, western painted turtles, and African sideneck turtles, among others. Turtles can be found in coastal waters, bays, lagoons, estuaries, and open seas. Turtles live on land, fresh water, and salt water. All turtles have their bodies enclosed in bony cartilage shells, but they can't leave their shell. The top and bottom shells develop from their rib and vertebral column and join together to form a skeletal box. Sea turtles cannot retract their limbs and head into their shell. Turtle species that can are classified into two groups: "sideneck" turtles that folds their neck to one side while retracting and "hidden neck" turtles that retract their head straight back into its shell.

Turtles are primarily omnivores, but some species, like tortoises, are herbivores. Omnivorous turtles that live in water eat jellyfish, squid, and sea vegetation. The green turtle primarily eats jellyfish. Tortoises eat only plants or invertebrates. Turtles have beaks which they use to grasp food. Hawksbills have a strong hawklike beak which they use to cut through sea sponges and coral. Turtles have no teeth, but loggerheads and alligator snapping turtles have powerful jaws that allow them to feed on fish, shellfish, and lobsters.

Tortoises are a species of land turtle that live exclusively on land. They share similar shells with other types of turtles but have columnar feet instead of the flipper-like limbs common to turtles. They live in habitats ranging from forests to deserts. Turtle hatchlings have so many threats that just one in a thousand survive to adulthood. Turtles that survive live comfortably for up to fifty years or more. Some sea turtles do not reach sexual maturity until they are fifty years old and typically live over seventy years.

Turtles vary in size, ranging up to two to seven feet long and weighing from 70 to over 1,500 pounds. The leatherback sea turtle is the largest sea turtle. It can weigh up to two thousand pounds.

Leatherback sea turtles don't have a hard shell. They travel a migratory distance of over ten thousand miles a year between their nesting and feeding grounds. The largest leatherback ever recorded measured nine feet long and weigh 2,138 pounds. Turtles don't have gills, so they need oxygen to breathe, but they can hold their breath for an extraordinary length of time. Sea turtles spend up to four to seven hours sleeping in water, and some turtles even hibernate in water. Turtles can dive long distances, up to three thousand feet, in search for jellyfish. Turtles come up to the water surface for air between lengthy dives to hunt for food. Drowning usually occurs when turtles get entangled in fishing gear and cannot escape for air.

If you ever get a chance to see a sea turtle out of the water, you may notice tears pouring out of its eyes. The sea turtle cries not because it is hurt or sad but because they need to get rid of excess salt in their body. Their tears are twice as salty as seawater. The tears clear sand from their eyes. Since sea turtles are attracted to light, they are guided home from the sea by the bright moonlight reflecting on the water. Human encroachment where sea turtles lay eggs introduces artificial lights that confuse them. Female sea turtles mate at sea and come to land to lay their eggs. They dig two-foot deep holes with their hind flippers and fertilize their eggs with sperm stored from earlier mating. Female turtles lay about 125 eggs per nest. The eggs mature within two months, and the newborns dig their way out of the nest and make their way to the sea.

Sea turtles are not very social. Once baby turtles break away, they stimulate others to do the same. This strength in numbers makes it possible for them to climb out of the deep nest and overpower certain predators on their way to the sea, and after hatchlings reach the water, they generally remain solitary until they mate. Turtles do not have maternal nurturing instincts. The female turtle takes care to protect her eggs by camouflaging the nest. Beyond that, they offer no special care for their hatchlings. After nesting, the turtles never return to check on their baby turtles.

Turtles are one of the few animals that eat seagrass, which helps to maintain seabed. Seagrass needs to be kept short so it can grow healthily and spread across the sand dunes. When turtles nest, not every egg will hatch. The unhatched eggs and discarded eggshells provide nutrients needed for dune vegetation. As dune vegetation grows, it prevents beach erosion. Turtle watching is a tourist attraction that provides economic growth and a source of income for coastal residents. Turtles face many dangers in their lifetime. While young, predators, such as fish, birds, snakes, and humans, prey on them. As adults, climate change and plastic pollution endanger them.

Wasps

The terms wasps, yellow jackets, and bees can be confusing. Basically, bees are herbivores as they eat nectar and collect pollen on their hair. Wasps, hornets, and yellow jackets on the other hand are hairless carnivores and eat bees and carry their prey by their feet. Although several European hornets have been spotted in the US, we do not have hornets in great numbers as the European hornets are only leftovers brought to the United States from Europe in the mid-1800s.

Wasps are hairless, narrow-waisted insects that sting. They build paper nests from wood pulp formed by their mouth parts and raise their young on insects. The most common wasps are the yellow jackets. Some wasps are predators and some are pollinators for either feeding themselves or supplying their nests. Solitary wasps parasitize almost every insect, making them valuable as pest controllers for many crops, such as tomatoes crops.

Only female wasps have stingers and can sting over and over. Female wasps don't die after a sting because their stinger remains in their bodies after pulling it out from the flesh after a sting. Their nests are relatively small with less than one hundred members in colonies. Although they feed on nectar, they feed insects to their young. Wasps are about one third of an inch to one-inch long. Hornets are larger. Wasps have black and yellow rings.

Female wasps will happily sting you if they think you're endangering their hive. You may think wasps live in hives as bees do, but that's not always the case. Some species of wasps, like yellow jackets and hornets, live in groups while others live alone. Interestingly, wasps use their stingers differently, depending on which type of environment they live in. Those who live in hives use their stingers to protect and defend their nests. On the other hand, wasps who live alone use their stingers for hunting prey.

Wasps like to hunt

If wasps weren't so aggressive with their stings, it would be beneficial to have them around our yards since they eat many other insects that we consider as pests.

Nest are like paper-mâché

Wasps rely on paper-thin wood fibers. By scraping away at wood, they create fragile flakes, which they can then mold into nests that resemble paper-mâché. That's why some wasps are referred to as paper wasps. Since wasps need wood fibers to build their nests, you're most likely to find them in attics, porches, and garage rafters. These places usually have exposed wooden beams which the wasps can carve.

Wasps are meat lovers

Although wasps may like sugar, if you've left your lemonade outside and unattended, wasps may leave it alone as they prefer to hunt other insects especially the insect larvae.

Males die after mating

The majority of wasps in any hive are female. The females are the workers who handle the task of running the hive. One female queen is in charge of laying new eggs. In late summer, any male wasps, called "drones," will mate with a few special females who will leave the nest and go on to start their own hives. Unfortunately for the drones, they will die after mating with the future queen.

Wasps use scent to communicate

When possible, you should avoid swatting a wasp. When wasps die, their body releases a chemical, and if other wasps are in the area, it will immediately alert them that a comrade has fallen and will make them more aggressive. If you happened to get rid of a wasp near its nest, you could soon have the whole hive swarming toward you in revenge for the death of their friend.

Wasps come in many colors

You're probably most familiar with the black-and-yellow variety of wasps, but wasps can come in just about any color you can imagine! The cuckoo wasp, or jewel wasp, of Australia, for example, is known for its metallic blue and green colors!

Underground nesters

The stinging wasp is black and yellow. Primarily yellow bands cover a dark abdomen. They begin their nests like the aerial nesters with an enveloped small comb made of wood fiber paper. Only these nests are started in soil depressions, rodent burrows, or in any small hole in the ground that will give protection until workers can develop. Once workers begin nest care, they enlarge the entrance hole and expand the nest. Combs are placed in tiers, one below the other. They can be very large; they have firm support from the soil surrounding the external envelope. Several species make their nests in building wall voids, attics, hollow trees, and other enclosed spaces as well as the ground.

Mud dauber wasps

Mud dauber wasps are not social wasps. They are in a different family group. Many paralyze spiders to build long clay mud cell tubes for their eggs. Dauber wasps are slender and either shiny black or brown, orange, or yellow in color with black markings. Many have long, slender-thread waists. Mud dauber wasps do not use a worker caste system. These wasps are not aggressive, and they will not sting unless they are threatened.

Mud daubers place their mud nests in protected places, such as attics, sheds, against house siding, and under porch overhangs. Many wasps congregate at the future site to construct their mud nests. Removal of these nests and repainting can be expensive. Mud daubers are easily controlled with pesticide aerosol contact sprays. After spraying, scrape away the mud nest and cover the area with a good quality paint.

Paper wasps

Queen paper wasps begin their nests by attaching a thick paper strand under an overhanging structure then build hollow paper cells by chewing wood or plant fibers mixed with water and shaped with her mouthparts. When about a half dozen cells are completed, the queen lays an egg near the bottom of each cell. The grubs that hatch from her eggs begin receiving nourishment from chewed-up bits of caterpillars from their mother's mouth parts. When they grow large enough to fill the cell cavity, they eventually pump out their wings and take their place as worker assistants to their mother. The common paper wasp with its umbrella-shaped nest best demonstrates the basic building pattern of a colony.

Management and control of paper wasps. Paper wasp nests are typically found near doorways and vacant areas. Wasps are attracted to fallen ripe fruits, such as apples and pears. Colonies in trees and buildings can be controlled by removing old nests and scrape the point of attachment, otherwise this attachment may be occupied by a new queen; and caulking all outside attic, window frames, and around wall openings.

Cicada wasp

Cicada (chee-kah-dah) wasps are yellow and black in color and are giant wasps more than one inch in length. Only female cicada wasps have stingers.

Why do wasps sting?

All wasps are capable of producing nasty stings, but they do not leave the stinger embedded in the skin, thus allowing wasps to sting many victims. Wasps are very protective of their nests and colonies and will attack if anyone approaches within a few feet of the nest. When a wasp stings, it injects a venomous fluid under the skin.

Wasp stings vs. bee stings

Most wasps stingers contain similar ingredients to bee stingers but different in the ingredient percentages. One of the main differences is the way wasps inject their venom. The wasp inserts its shaft into the victim, and the barbs quickly move forward and backward like a sawing action. The barbs have backward-pointed hooks along their edges. As the shaft moves deeper into the skin, the pumping action causes poison venom to pump through the shaft and into the victim.

Both bees and wasps use a similar process, but the bee is unable to remove its shaft out from the skin because its barbs become imbedded and can't be removed. The stinger then gets pulled out of its abdomen, causing the bee to later die. The wasp stinger has very small barbs and can extract their shaft from the skin then fly off.

Yellow Jackets

Yellow jackets are more aggressive than wasps or hornets and are more likely to sting. The pain from a yellow jacket sting is less than that from a wasp or a hornet. Yellow jackets have a smooth stinger, which allows them to sting over and over. In Colorado, it was estimated that yellow jackets caused at least 90 percent of the bee stings in this state. Some yellow jacket nests hang down from trees and shrubs while others are constructed underground. Yellow jackets feed their young on flies and caterpillars.

Yellow jackets are black with yellow markings on the front of the head and yellow around the abdomen. The face is primarily yellow with dark eyes. Front wings are folded lengthwise when at rest. Yellow jackets' closest relatives, the hornets, closely resemble them but have a much bigger head. Yellow jackets typically visit to picnic areas and parks during the summer as they are attracted to meat, fruit, and sweet drinks.

The yellow jacket diet

Yellow jackets are carnivorous, primarily feeding on other insects like flies and bees. However, they also feed on fruits and nectar. Yellow jackets will travel as far as one mile away from their nest to search for food.

Yellow jacket behavior

Yellow jackets are social insects and live in large colonies. The queen, drones, and worker all have specific tasks to help support the colony. The queen lays hundreds of eggs, the drones fertilize a receptive queen, and workers do the tasks needed to operate and maintain the colony.

Nest building

In the spring, the yellow jacket queen collects wood fiber to make her nest. The nest is constructed of paperlike material made from chewed wood fibers mixed with saliva. Some species build the nest underground while others build nests around houses. The nest contains cells that look like a honeybee's comb. The nest is started by a single queen. New nests are typically built every year because the abandoned nest is often destroyed by birds searching for food.

Aerial yellow jackets

Aerial yellow jackets are found in western and eastern United States and in Canada. This species begins their nests in March or April and completed by the end of July. After this time, aerial yellow jackets are no longer active. Their nests are generally attached to building overhangs. They are smaller than those of similar species. After they are no longer active, set the ladder and cut the nest down and seal them in a plastic bag. Spray the nest with pesticide. The queen, workers, and larvae will die.

Eastern yellow jacket

This ground-nesting yellow jacket is found in the eastern half of the United States. Workers are slightly smaller than most yellow jackets. Colony size can be around five thousand. The nest is dark tan, made of partially decomposed wood, and is quite brittle. Most yellow jackets have slightly barbed stingers which often remain in the flesh when the insect is slapped off.

North American yellow jacket

The North American yellow jacket nests in attics and wall voids. Workers can chew through ceilings and walls and enter into adjacent rooms. The nest is made of strong light gray paper. Colonies may be active in protected voids into November and December.

Yellow jackets management

Problems encountered with yellow jackets occur when humans step on or contact a colony entrance. Workers no longer feed larvae in the late summer months. Instead, they search for nectar, juices, fallen fruit, and other places where humans gather.

When yellow jackets visit wet manure and sewage, they pick up bacteria and stingers. In essence, the stinger becomes a hypodermic needle and inject the bacteria into the victim's skin. Blood poisoning may occur after being stung by a yellow jacket.

Habitat

Manage outdoor food by cleaning garbage cans regularly and use tight lids. Empty cans daily especially prior to periods of heavy human traffic at zoos, amusement parks, fairs, and sporting events. Remove bakery items, sweets, soft drink cans, and candy wrappers several times a day during periods of yellow jacket activity.

Studies show that stings were dramatically reduced when drinks are served in cups with lids. Locate trash cans away from food areas. To limit yellow jacket exposure in wall voids and attics, caulk and screen all openings.

Yellow jackets pesticide application

I avoid destroying insects, when possible, but when they nest close to home and become a threat, I spray the nest after dark then remove it.

Transit System

Imagine trying to drive around Boston without the transit systems? Or imagine if 90 percent of the roads throughout Boston didn't exist? That's the type of problem pollinators have! The United Kingdom has a solution to this problem of the loss of flowers for pollinators. They have a series of insect pathways called the B-Line, running adjacent to roads through many towns. The B-Line links existing wildlife areas together, creating a network, like a commuter transit system, that weave across UK towns.

Wildlife Webcams

Here's an interesting live wildlife cam website. At this site, you will be able to select many different webcams: *http://sportsmanspara-diseonline.com.*

Worms

Typical earthworms do not have eyes but instead have sensitive organs and rely on vibrations felt through their body to travel and to avoid prey. Worms have very strong mouth muscles but do not have teeth. Earthworms eat their weight in decayed insects, decayed animals, as well as organic matter in soil. They often surface at night to pull fallen leaves into their burrow. They inhale and exhale through their skin and require humid conditions.

Although they do not mate, they can produce about two per year because their organs are of both sexes. They travel below the frost level in winter to avoid freezing. Worms hibernate at freezing temperatures. However, if frozen, they will not survive. Despite popular belief, worms do not surface during heavy rain to avoid drowning. In fact, they travel greater distance during this time than having to navigate through soil. Their life span is about four to eight years.

Chapter 6

Thoughts from Astronomy

Introduction

How much do we know to fully appreciate astronomy? Although most of us may like to know more, what we do know is perhaps enough to assure us that astronomy is beyond amazing.

In this chapter, I not only provide a source for our reference libraries, but more importantly, I hope to reveal some of the amazing concepts about astronomy that will help trigger our thoughts and guide our lives toward positive directions.

Coriolis Effect

Suppose you are standing at the equator and you throw a ball due north to your friend in the middle of Michigan. If you throw the ball high and in a straight line, it will appear to land to the right of your friend because since he is at a higher latitude where Earth's rotation is slower than at the equator, he is moving slower and cannot catch up to the ball. Now let's suppose you're standing on the North Pole. From your perspective on the North Pole, when you throw the ball to the same friend, the ball would appear to land to the right of him. But this time, it's because your friend is moving faster than you and has moved ahead of the ball. This apparent deflection is referred to as the Coriolis effect, which was described by the French engineer and mathematician Gustave Gaspard Coriolis in 1835. Fluids and air moving across large areas are affected by Earth's rotation similar to the path of the ball. The direction of the Coriolis effect behaves opposite in the southern hemisphere.

As warm air at the equator rises, it flows toward the poles and deflected to the right as they move northward. These air currents return to the ground when they reach higher and cooler latitudes then gradually flow back toward the equator. Fast-moving objects, such as airplanes and rockets, are influenced by the Coriolis effect, and this effect needs to be taken into account when traveling over long distances.

You can simulate and observe the Coriolis effect with you and a friend sitting across from one another on a typical counterclockwise rotating merry-go-round while attempting to throw a ball back and forth. Although the ball will travel straight, it will appear to curve to the right of your friend, and he will miss the ball every time because he is still moving while the ball is in the air. Only ground observers would see the ball as traveling straight.

Hurricanes

The Coriolis effect plays a major role in the development of hurricanes. Rising warm air above tropical waters form high pressure areas and cloud formations. Due to the Coriolis effect the cloud formations encircle and attempt to enter a relatively low-pressure area to neutralize pressures. The low-pressure area eventually becomes the "eye" of the hurricane. These cloud formations rotate in a counterclockwise direction around the low-pressure area in the northern hemisphere and clockwise in the southern hemisphere.

Earth's Trip Around the Sun

Earth's 23.5-degree tilt from its axis is the cause for Earth's four seasons. Beginning at winter solstice on December 21, Earth's northern hemisphere is colder because it faces the sun at an angle while the southern hemisphere is warmer because it faces the sun more directly. Then on March 21, Earth's orbit reaches the vernal equinox where both the northern and southern hemispheres face the sun directly and, therefore, daytime and nighttime hours are of equal length. Then on June 21, Earth's orbit reaches summer solstice. Earth's northern hemisphere is warmer because it faces the sun more directly while the southern hemisphere is colder because it faces the sun at an angle. Then on September 21, Earth's orbit reaches the autumnal equinox where both the northern and southern hemispheres once again face the sun's angle more directly and, therefore, daytime and nighttime hours are of equal length.

Earth's orbit then approaches winter solstice at which time 365 days completes one Earth orbit around the sun. The acceptable traditional beginning first days of the four seasons occur on the dates of the two solstices and the two equinoxes. However, I believe that seasons begin at the midpoints of solstices and equinoxes. Using a clock for my analogy, let's assume that twelve is winter December 21, the three on the clock is spring March 21, six is summer June 21, and the nine is fall September 21, then back to the twelve for winter, and this completes one year of 365 days or one Earth's orbit around the sun. Conventional wisdom has us to believe that December 21 is the first day of winter, right? If so, is December 24 the third day of winter? Is March 20 the last day of winter? I believe that winter occurs only on one day December 21, and moments thereafter, we are approaching spring. Assuming one's birthday is on February 10 and he or she turned fifty years old, is he still fifty years old on February 11? I say no; he is approaching fifty-one. Turning fifty or being fifty is over, and it's history. He has one birthday a year on February 10, and every day thereafter places him closer to fifty-one. This reminds me of the opening line of Tom T. Hall's classic song "(Old Dogs and Children and) Watermelon Wine." "How old do you think I am," he said / I said, "Well, I didn't know." / He said, "I turned 65 about 11 months ago."

The clock tells me that winter is at the twelve mark, and every day thereafter spring gets closer. Spring is at the three mark and so on. Traditionally, in many temperate regions, winter solstice (the twelve mark) is considered the middle of winter. Only one day is winter. Days prior are approaching winter; days after are approaching spring. Earth's orbit around the sun covers approximately 580 million miles in 365 days at a speed of approximately sixty-six thousand miles per hour. The planet with the least amount of tilt is Mercury at 0 degrees. The greatest amount of tilt is the planet Venus at 177.3 degrees.

Blue skies

All colors (wavelengths) emitted from sunlight are absorbed in dust particles and air molecules except blue. Daytime sky is, therefore, blue because molecules in the air scatter blue light from the sun more than they scatter red light. The color blue appears on the ultraviolet end of the color spectrum and is opposite from the infrared end of the color spectrum.

Red sunsets

When we look toward the west during a sunset, we see red and orange colors because the blue light has been scattered out and away from our line of sight. When the moon is overhead, it goes through about ten miles of tropospheric air. But when the moon is on the horizon, it goes through about 290 miles through the troposphere! That's not only enough to scatter away most of the blue light, but it also scatters away about 99 percent of *the total* light that comes from the sun!

So typically, only the red light passes through. This phenomenon not only explains why the sky looks red at sunset; it also explains why *the sun looks red during a lunar eclipse*! The only light that passes through is the small amount of red light that makes itself all the way through Earth's atmosphere and onto Earth. The color red appears on the infrared end of the color spectrum and opposite from the ultraviolet end.

Eclipses

Lunar eclipse

During a lunar eclipse, the full moon cannot be seen for about three hours because it passes across Earth's shadow. A lunar eclipse can only occur during a full moon phase and during the night when all three bodies of the moon, Earth, and sun are in line and Earth is physically between the sun and the moon, thus casting its shadow onto the moon. Despite the sun's diameter of approximately 864,938 miles, the moon's diameter of approximately 2,160 miles, the earth's diameter of approximately eight thousand miles and the distances between each body, it's amazing that Earth's shadow cast on the moon turns out to be the same diameter as the moon.

Solar eclipse

During a solar eclipse, the sun cannot be seen for about seven minutes because the new moon phase passes between the sun and Earth, thus blocking sunlight from reaching Earth. This can only occur during the day and during a new moon phase when all three bodies of sun, moon, and Earth are in line.

Equinoxes

Vernal equinox

Vernal (spring) equinox occurs when the sun is directly above the equator on March 21 or 22 during Earth's orbit around the sun. The number of daytime and nighttime hours are of equal length and thus the name equinox. At vernal equinox, Earth is beyond the winter solstice in December and orbiting toward the summer solstice in June.

Autumnal equinox

Autumnal (fall) equinox occurs when the sun is directly above the equator on September 21 or 22 during Earth's orbit around the sun. The number of daytime and nighttime hours are of equal length and thus the name equinox. At autumnal equinox, Earth is beyond the summer solstice in June and is orbiting toward the winter solstice in December.

The sun rises due east and sets due west only on two days of the year on the spring equinox, March 21, and on the fall equinox,

September 21. In fact, the events of the equinoxes and solstice occur only momentarily. For as soon as time arrives for these events, time departs.

On all remaining 363 days of the year, the sun rises either north of due east or south of due east, depending on Earth's orbital direction, and sets north of due west or south of due west, also depending on Earth's orbital direction.

Each day, the rising and the setting points of the sun changes slightly, then the sun slows down and appears to stop at the solstices (meaning solar still or sun stops) on December 21 and June 21 to reverses direction toward its respective equinox. Although it appears that the sun is responsible for these motions, the sun is relatively stationary, it's Earth's rotation and orbit around the sun which causes these effects.

Moon

The moon's orbit around Earth generally follows the path above Earth's equator. From the northern hemisphere, the moon appears to travel slightly south of this path, while in the southern hemisphere, the moon appears to travel north of this path. Here are some interesting facts about our moon. All numbers are approximate.

Closest to Earth: 225,623 miles (perigee)
Diameter: 2,158 miles
Farthest from Earth: 252,088 miles (apogee)
Magnetic field: Yes
Orbit miles: 239,000 miles around Earth
Orbit speed: 2,288 miles per hour
Orbits Earth: 27 Earth days
Rotation speed: 10 miles per hour
Temperature: 260°F day and -279°F night

Orbit direction

Although our moon orbits Earth counterclockwise from west to east, it appears to be traveling from east to west because Earth rotates counterclockwise faster from west to east than the moon orbits Earth. Consider this analogy: suppose you are a passenger in a westbound automobile traveling at twenty miles per hour and you look out your side window and see a pedestrian walking five miles per hour also westbound. As you pass the pedestrian, he appears to be walking eastbound!

That's because you are traveling faster than the pedestrian. Using another example, suppose you are driving on a rural road at about twenty miles per hour and you pass a bicyclist traveling in the same direction but much slower. While passing the bicyclist, it would appear that the bicyclist was traveling in the opposite direction. That may not be too obvious since the front of the bicycle implies the direction of travel. However, in this scenario, suppose the bicycle were a ball about three feet in diameter and suspended three feet above the pavement. Now while passing this ball, the ball would appear to be traveling in the opposite direction…without any doubt. But the only way you would know for sure would be if you were to come to a complete stop.

We see only one side of the moon

The moon rotates on its axis in approximately every twenty-seven days and also orbits Earth in approximately every twenty-seven days. This phenomenon is called "tidal locking" and is why the moon displays only one side to the Earth. But how? Here's an analogy that I use to demonstrate this situation. Suppose you are the planet Earth and you are standing in the center of your living room. And suppose your neighbor Joanne is the moon and she is also standing in your living room but ten feet away from you. Both you and Joanne must maintain eye contact without moving your heads. Now ask Joanne to slowly walk around you in a counterclockwise circle while still maintaining the ten-foot distance from you and while still maintaining eye contact with you. Use your feet to rotate your body while remaining in one spot and while maintaining eye contact with Joanne during her orbit around you. After Joanne has completed her orbit, you will notice that both of you were always facing each other, and you *never* saw Joanne's back! Joanne, therefore, must have been rotating in order to maintain eye contact with you during her orbit. In that respect, Earth and moon are synchronized so that Earth always sees only one side of the Moon. Now using the same exercise, if you (planet Earth) were to rotate in your spot a little faster, Joanne (moon) would then appear to be moving in the opposite direction.

Moon phases

The same half of the moon always faces the Earth. During moon's orbit around the Earth, the phase or angle between the moon and the sun will determine the amount of the moon's surface that will be lit by the sun and reflected to Earth. The moon goes through four major phases, or angles, to the sun and four minor phases. There are several days between each of the major and each of the minor moon phase angles and approximately twenty-seven days to complete one moon orbit around the Earth.

Observing the Earth from above the North Pole, the moon orbits the Earth in a counterclockwise direction from west to east while Earth also rotates counterclockwise from west to east. However, since Earth rotates faster than the moon orbits, the moon, therefore, appears to move in the opposite direction from east to west! If Earth were to stop rotating, we would clearly see that the moon rises from the west and sets to the east. However, it's common practice to simply say the moon rises from the east and sets to the west. The eight phases of the Moon listed below are all in Eastern Standard Time.

Phase 1: New moon. The new moon is a major phase located in line between the sun and Earth, and, therefore, invisible. The new moon occurs only during the daytime. It rises around sunrise, transits overhead around twelve noon, and sets around sunset. This moon marks the beginning of the moon phases on its counterclockwise orbit around Earth. Thus the name "new moon."

New moon phase

Phase 2: Waxing crescent moon. After the new moon passes, the minor phase waxing crescent moon begins to appear. The bright area of this moon is becoming bigger (waxing). This moon rises in the east horizon about 9:00 AM, transits overhead around 3:00 PM and sets in the west horizon about 9:00 PM.

Waxing crescent moon phase

Phase 3: First quarter moon. After the waxing crescent moon passes, the major phase first quarter moon begins to appear. At its peak, half the area of this moon is bright while its other half is dark, and thus the name "half moon." This moon rises in the east horizon about twelve noon, transits overhead about 6:00 PM, and sets in the west horizon about twelve midnight.

First quarter moon phase

Phase 4: Waxing gibbous moon. After the first quarter moon passes, the minor phase waxing gibbous moon begins to appear. At its peak, over half the area of this moon is bright (gibbous). It rises in the east horizon around 3:00 PM, transits overhead around 9:00 PM, and sets at the west horizon about 3:00 AM.

Waxing gibbous moon phase

Phase 5: Full moon. After the waxing gibbous moon passes, the major phase full moon begins to appear. The Earth is between the moon and the sun with all three bodies in line, and therefore, this moon can only be seen at night. At its peak, this moon is fully lit, rises in the east horizon about sunset, transits overhead about twelve midnight, and sets in the west horizon around sunrise.

Full moon phase

Phase 6: Waning gibbous moon. After the full moon passes, the minor phase waning gibbous moon begins to appear. The dark area of this moon is becoming bigger (gibbous). At its peak, this moon rises in the east horizon around 9:00 PM, transits overhead around 3:00 AM, and sets in the west horizon about 9:00 AM.

Waning gibbous moon phase

Phase 7: Third quarter moon. After the waning gibbous moon passes, the major phase third quarter moon begins to appear. At its peak, the light and dark areas are equal. This moon is commonly referred to as the half moon. It rises in the east horizon around twelve midnight, transits overhead about 6:00 AM, and sets in the west horizon around twelve noon.

Third quarter moon phase

Phase 8: Waning crescent moon. After the third quarter moon passes, the minor phase waning crescent moon begins to appear. At its peak, over half of this moon area is dark. This moon rises in the east horizon at about 3:00 AM, transits overhead about 9:00 AM, and sets in the west horizon around 3:00 PM.

Waning crescent moon phase

Table summary

Moon Phase	Approx. Angle to the Sun	Approx. Moonlit Surface	Approx. Time Moon Rises in East	Approx. Transits Overhead	Approx. Time Moon Sets in West
New	0 Degrees	0 Percent	Sunrise	12 Noon	Sunset
Waxing Crescent	45 Degrees	25 Percent	9:00 AM	3:00 PM	9:00 PM
First Quarter	90 Degrees	50 Percent	12 Noon	6:00 PM	12 Midnight
Waxing Gibbous	135 Degrees	75 Percent	3:00 PM	9:00 PM	3:00 AM
Full	180 Degrees	100 Percent	Sunset	12 Midnight	Sunrise
Waning Gibbous	225 Degrees	75 Percent	9:00 PM	3:00 AM	9:00 AM
Third Quarter	270 Degrees	50 Percent	12 Midnight	6:00 AM	12 Noon
Waning Crescent	315 Degrees	25 Percent	3:00 AM	9:00 AM	3:00 PM

Except for the new moon and full moon phases, all other moon phases are excellent for viewing through a telescope. The bright areas of these phases cast long shadows on the moon's surface, revealing astonishing details. However, I find that the waxing crescent, waning gibbous, waxing gibbous, and the waning crescent moon phases produce the most vivid surface details because the brightness areas are minimum and therefore cast the long shadows.

What's a blue moon?

A blue moon is when two full moons occur in one month. In such a situation, the second moon is referred to as the blue moon. There are typically twelve full moons each year. However, due to the timing of the moon orbiting the Earth, along with other phenomena, there will be such an occurrence every two or three years whereby one year will have thirteen full moons.

Other than many historical myths and folklore, the moon is not blue and doesn't appear very often, thus the expression or cliché "once in a blue moon."

Fire on the moon?

There is no atmosphere on the moon and therefore no oxygen to start a fire.

Summary

For those having difficulty understanding moon phases, while the moon is orbiting Earth and while Earth is rotating, consider this: suppose Earth suddenly stopped rotating but the moon continued to orbit Earth counterclockwise and you had previously placed an observer at 90 degrees from you 1/4 way around the Earth, a second observer at 180 degrees from you 1/2 way around the Earth, and a third observer at 270 degrees from you 3/4 way around the Earth. Now during a new moon overhead at your location, the observer at 90 degrees would report a first quarter moon phase overhead, the observer at 180 degrees would report a full moon phase overhead, and the observer at 270 degrees would report a third quarter moon phase overhead.

Planets

While looking at celestial bodies on a clear dark night, are there ways to tell whether we are looking at a planet or a star? Yes, we can tell the difference between a planet and a star. A star will twinkle because it's light-years away, and its light passes through an enormous amount of atmosphere which bends light causing a twinkle effect. Planets, on the other hand, are much closer, and there is less atmosphere between you and the planet, so they don't twinkle. However, when a planet is close to the horizon, there's more atmosphere in the line of sight to the planet, and so planets can twinkle. Also, stars are fixed in the night sky. Although the rotation of the earth causes stars to appear in different locations during the night, stars still possess the same relative distance apart.

All planets orbit around the sun counterclockwise, and since their orbital speed and distance from the sun are different from one another, they will appear in different locations. There are a total of nine planets in our solar system, including Pluto. Four planets are considered inner planets while five are considered outer planets. The inner planets are Mercury, Venus, Earth, and Mars. Outer planets are Jupiter, Saturn, Uranus, Neptune, and Pluto.

Mercury: first planet from the sun

The surface gravity on Mercury is only about 38 percent of the surface gravity on Earth. So if you weigh one hundred pounds on Earth, you will weigh thirty-eight pounds on Mercury.

Here are the approximate characteristics of Mercury:

Atmosphere: None
Axis tilt: 0 degrees
Diameter: 3,000 miles (less than half the size of Earth)
Distance from the sun: 36 million miles
Magnetic field: Yes
Moons: None
Orbital distance: 29 million miles around the sun
Orbital speed: 107,000 miles per hour
Orbits the sun: 88 Earth days (faster than any other planet)
Rings: None
Rotation speed: CCW at 7 miles per hour around its equator
Rotation time: 176 Earth days
Surface: Rocky
Surface gravity: 38 percent less than Earth
Temperatures: -280°F at night and 800°F at day

Venus: second planet from the sun

The former Soviet Union landed eight unmanned spaceships on Venus including landings on December 15, 1970; in 1972; on October 22, 1975; on December 1978; and in March 1982. The surface gravity on Venus is about 91 percent of the surface gravity on Earth. If you weigh one hundred pounds on Earth, you will weigh about ninety-one pounds on Venus. Venus is the brightest planet because its closest to Earth.

Here are the approximate characteristics of Venus:

Atmosphere: Thick, ninety times the pressure on Earth
Axis tilt: 177.3 degrees
Diameter: 7,500 miles
Distance from the sun: 67 million miles, average
Magnetic field: None
Moons: None
Orbital distance: 67 million miles, average
Orbital speed: 78,300 miles per hour
Orbits the sun: 225 Earth days
Rings: None
Rotation speed: CW at 4 miles per hour around its equator
Rotation time: 243 Earth days
Surface: Rocky
Surface gravity: 91 percent of the gravity on Earth
Temperature: 850°F day and night

Earth: third planet from the sun

Here are the approximate characteristics of Earth:

Atmosphere: Gas
Axis tilt: 23.5 degrees
Diameter: 8,000 miles
Distance from the sun: 93 million miles, average
Magnetic field: Yes

Moons: One
Orbital distance: 580 million miles, average
Orbital speed: 66,000 miles per hour
Orbits the sun: 365 days
Rings: None
Rotation speed: CCW at 1,000 miles per hour around its equator
Rotation time: 24 hours
Surface: Rocky
Surface gravity: Yes
Temperatures: 60°F average

Mars: fourth planet from the sun

Mars does not have an atmosphere except very close to its surface. No magnetic field to protect against solar particles. The giant sticky dust storms from the mountain's red area causes temperature difference between the surface and the air. Dust blocks the sun while sand blows and rubs together causing lightning. Gravity is about one third that of Earth. If you weigh 150 pounds on Earth, you will weigh about 50 pounds on Mars. Lava from years ago forms cavities, and because of the low gravity, lava formations remain mostly on the surface while tunnels are formed below the toxic surface. No oxygen however; ice caps can make water.

Since all resources on Earth are being used up, additional number of asteroids are threatening our planet, and global warming is a continued threat to our planet, Mars may be our only lifeboat. Plans to visit Mars is scheduled for the 2030s.

Here are the approximate characteristics of Mars:

Atmosphere: Gas
Axis tilt: 25 degrees
Diameter: 4,200 miles
Distance from the sun: 141 million miles, average
Magnetic field: None

Moons: Two moons:
- Phobos (fear)
- Deimos (dread)

Orbital distance: 142 million miles
Orbital speed: 54,000 miles per hour
Orbits the sun: 687 Earth days
Rings: None
Rotation speed: CCW at 538 miles per hour around its equator
Rotation time: 25 hours Earth time
Surface: Iron, nickel, sulfur
Surface gravity: 1/3 of Earth's gravity
Temperature: -85°F average, -250 at poles

Jupiter: fifth planet from the sun

Due to the enormous size of Jupiter, it is estimated that Jupiter may have well over two hundred moons of which the majority have yet to be confirmed. The gravity on Jupiter is about 2.4 times greater than on Earth. So if you weigh 150 pounds on Earth, you will weigh 360 pounds on Jupiter.

Here are the approximate characteristics of Jupiter:

Atmosphere: Gas
Axis tilt: 3.13 degrees
Diameter: 87,000 miles; every planet can fit in Jupiter, plus!
Distance from the sun: 484 million miles, average
Magnetic field: Yes, strong
Moons: 92 moons; the four moons of Galileo are also the largest moons orbiting Jupiter:
- Europa
- Io (nearest to Jupiter)
- Ganymede (largest moon in our solar system)
- Callisto (second largest moon of Jupiter)

Orbital distance: 484 million miles
Orbital speed: 29,000 miles per hour
Orbits the sun: 11.86 Earth years

Rings: Four rings:
- Thick inner ring named Halo
- Thin and bright main ring
- Two faint outer rings

Rotation speed: CCW at 28,324 miles per hour around its equator
Rotation time: 10 Earth time
Surface: Gas
Surface gravity: 2.4 times Earth's gravity
Temperature: -238°F average

Saturn: sixth planet from the sun

There are thousands of rings around Saturn (similar to the grooves around a vinyl record). Seven of the Saturn's moons travel within these rings and hold the rings together. However, there are a total of more than ninety moons around Saturn, but that amount often changes. The moon Edey is more than two million miles from Saturn and orbits Saturn in the clockwise direction opposite the orbits of its other moons. Edey always faces Saturn as it is locked in that position. This moon has a rough ring around its circumference because its backside gathers solar dust, and as a result, it distorts other rings as it orbits Saturn.

There are severe windstorms on Saturn. Rain is formed by ice particles within the rings and drawn into Saturn by the gas giant's magnetic field. There's a hexagonal-shaped area directly around Saturn's north pole with a whirlpool vortex in its center. The sides of the hexagon are approximately nine thousand miles longer than Earth's diameter.

The diameter of the hexagon is about 18,000 miles, and the height is about 190 miles high. *Voyager* first discovered Saturn's hexagon in 1981, then the hexagon was photographed by the *Cassini* (named for Italian astronomer Giovanni Domenico Cassini) spacecraft in 2006 and studied.

Here are the approximate characteristics of Saturn:

Atmosphere: Thin gas

Axis tilt: 26.7 degrees
Diameter: 72,000 miles
Distance from the sun: 888 million miles, average
Magnetic field: Yes
Moons: More than 140 moons; the surface of the Titan moon is covered with sand dunes
Orbital distance: 887 million miles around the sun
Orbital speed: 21,600 miles per hour
Orbits the sun: 29.45 Earth years
Rings: Seven
Rotation speed: CCW at 22,891 miles per hour around its equator
Rotation time: About 11 Earth hours
Surface: Gas
Surface gravity: About the same as the gravity on Earth
Temperature: -220°F

Uranus: seventh planet from the sun

The gravity on Uranus is slightly less than that on Earth. If you weigh one hundred pounds on Earth, you will weigh about ninety pounds on Uranus.

Here are the approximate characteristics of Uranus:

Atmosphere: Gas
Axis tilt: 98 degrees
Diameter: 31,700 miles
Distance from the sun: 1.78 billion miles, average
Magnetic field: Yes
Moons: Twenty-seven
- Ariel
- Belinda
- Bianca
- Caliban
- Cordelia
- Cressida
- Cupid

- Desdemona
- Ferdinand
- Francisco
- Juliet
- Mab
- Margaret
- Miranda
- Oberon
- Ophelia
- Perdita
- Portia
- Prospero
- Puck
- Rosalind
- Setebos
- Stephano
- Sycorax
- Titania
- Trinculo
- Umbriel

Orbital distance: 1.8 billion miles around the sun
Orbital speed: 15,290 miles per hour
Orbits the sun: 84 earth years
Rings: Two sets
- 9 inner rings
- 2 outer rings

Rotation speed: CW at 14,794 miles per hour around its equator
Rotation time: 17 hours and 14 minutes Earth time
Surface: Gas
Surface gravity: Slightly less than the gravity on Earth
Temperature: -320°F

Neptune: eighth planet from the sun

The gravity on Neptune is about 114 percent greater than the gravity on Earth. If you weigh one hundred pounds on Earth, you will weigh about 114 pounds on Neptune.

Here are the approximate characteristics of Neptune:

Atmosphere: Gas
Axis tilt: 28.5 degrees
Diameter: 31,000 miles
Distance from the sun: 2.80 billion miles, average
Magnetic field: Yes, strong
Moons: Thirteen
  • Despina
  • Galatea
  • Halimede
  • Laomedeia
  • Larissa
  • Naiad
  • Nereid
  • Neso
  • Proteus
  • Psamathe
  • Sao
  • Thalassa
  • Triton
Orbital distance: 2.8 billion miles around the sun
Orbital speed: 21,146 miles per hour
Orbits the sun: 164.79 Earth years
Rings: Five rings
  • Galle
  • Leverrier
  • Lassell
  • Arago
  • Adams
Rotation speed: CCW at 12,000 miles per hour around its equator

Rotation time: 16 hours and 6 minutes Earth time
Surface: Gas
Surface gravity: 114 percent greater than Earth's gravity
Temperature: -353°F

Pluto: ninth planet from the sun

Pluto is the only planet in our solar system that rotates counterclockwise. The surface gravity on Pluto is about one-twelfth the surface gravity on Earth. If you weigh one hundred pounds on Earth, you will weigh eight pounds on Pluto. NASA flew past Pluto in 2015 using the *New Horizons* spacecraft and spotted a bright heart shape on its surface at lower right.

Pluto's heart
(Photo courtesy of NASA)

Here are the approximate characteristics of Pluto:

Atmosphere: Thin gas
Axis tilt: 119.61 degrees

Diameter: 1,500 Miles
Distance from the sun: 3.70 billion miles, average
Magnetic field: None
Moons: Five moons:
- Charon—Charon is half the size of Pluto and is tidally locked with Pluto.
- Hydra
- Kerberos
- Nix
- Styk

Orbital distance: 19 billion miles around the sun
Orbital speed: 10,379 miles per hour
Orbits the sun: 248 Earth years
Rings: None
Rotation speed: CW at 1/4 of the speed around Earth's equator
Rotation time: 6.5 Earth days
Surface: Ice and rock
Surface gravity: 1/12th of the gravity on Earth
Temperature: -385°F to -369°F

Planet sizes

This list shows approximate diameter for each planet from the smallest to the largest.

- Pluto—1,500 miles
- Mercury—3,000 miles
- Mars—4,200 miles
- Venus—7,500 miles
- Earth—7,900 miles
- Neptune—31,000 miles
- Uranus—31,700 miles
- Saturn—72,000 miles
- Jupiter—87,000 miles

Planet records

Although many celestial conditions may alter the results, the following list shows some typical records of all the planets:

- Axis tilt
  Greatest: Venus
  Smallest: Mercury
- Brightness
  Most: Venus
  Least: Neptune
- Diameter
  Largest: Jupiter
  Smallest: Mercury and Pluto
- Distance from the sun
  Farthest: Neptune
  Shortest: Mercury
- Moons
  Most: Jupiter
  Least: Mercury and Venus
- Orbital distance
  Longest: Neptune
  Shortest: Mercury
- Orbital speed
  Fastest: Mercury
  Slowest: Pluto
- Orbits the sun
  Most Earth days: Jupiter
  Least Earth days: Mercury
- Rings:
  Most: Saturn
  Least: Mercury, Venus, Earth, Mars, Pluto
- Rotation speed
  Fastest: Jupiter
  Slowest: Venus
- Rotation time

Longest: Venus
Shortest: Mars
- Temperature (average)
Hottest: Venus
Coldest: Uranus
- Rotation speed
Fastest: Jupiter
Slowest: Venus

Universe

There are two major phenomena in our universe called (1) dark energy, which tends to expand space by pushing everything away, and (2) dark matter, which tends to bring everything in space close together. Dark matter is getting bigger. The universe is over thirteen billion years old and has a diameter spanning over 150 billion light-years. Based on Einstein's general theory of relativity, the universe may take on three shapes: open, closed, or flat. Further, it was confirmed that the universe is flat.

Solstice

Summer solstice

Summer solstice occurs when Earth is farthest from the sun (aphelion) during Earth's orbit around the sun. However, Earth's tilt allows the northern hemisphere to face the sun's rays more directly on June 21 (or 22); thus the northern hemisphere is warmer while the southern hemisphere is colder and the daytime hours are long while the nighttime hours are short. Earth's northern hemisphere has reached its maximum exposure to the sun and begins its journey toward autumnal equinox in March.

Winter solstice

Winter solstice occurs when Earth is closest to the sun (perihelion) during Earth's orbit around the sun. Earth's tilt allows the northern hemisphere to face the sun's rays at its maximum angle on December 21 (or 22); thus the northern hemisphere is colder while the southern hemisphere is warmer and nighttime hours are long while daytime hours are short. Earth's northern hemisphere has reached its minimal exposure to the sun and begins its journey toward vernal equinox in September.

What's a Light-Year?

A light-year is not a time frame. It's a measure of distance from any lighted object to our eyes. This includes everything in the universe from all objects on the ground to all celestial bodies and based on the speed of light. Celestial bodies are so far away from Earth that in order to deal with their astronomically large numbers, we use light-years. What constitutes a light-year? Since light travels at approximately 180,000 miles per second, we need to multiply the speed of light by the number of seconds in one year.

So how many seconds are there in one year? There are 6 seconds in 1 minute, times 60 minutes in 1 hour, times 24 hours in 1 day, times 365 days in 1 year, comes to 31,536,000 seconds in 1 year or 5,676,480,000,000 miles (rounded to six trillion miles) for one light-year!

Formula

> 1 Light-year = (Speed of light) × (Number of seconds in 1 year)
> 1 Light-year = (180,000 miles per second) × (31,536,000)
> 1 Light-year = 5,676,480,000,000 miles, rounded to 6 trillion miles

We can determine the number of miles a star is from our sun by multiplying the miles in one light-year by the number of light-years to the star. So if a star is 2 million light-years from the sun,

2 million light-years times 6 trillion miles per 1 light-year equals the distance of 1.2 followed by nineteen zeros miles away from the sun. The closest galaxy to Earth is the Andromeda galaxy, which is 2.5 million light-years away or a mileage distance of 1.5 followed by nineteen zeros! Yes, it's much easier to say that Andromeda galaxy is 2.5 million light-years away from the sun than to say it's 150,000,000,000,000,000,000 miles away!

Proxima Centauri (meaning nearest) is the closest star at 4.24 light-years away from our sun. A light-year is six trillion miles from the sun. It would take about 950 million years to walk to Proxima. Earendel star is in the Cetus constellation discovered by the Hubble Space Telescope in 2022. Earendel is about 28 billion light-years away, between fifty and five hundred times as big as our sun and millions of times brighter.

How are light-years determined? How can we know distances to stars? Well, there is no easy method to measure distances to stars from Earth. However, astronomers use the brightness and color spectrum of stars close to Earth and can measure their distances to some degree of accuracy. Then by observing the brightness and color spectrum of distant stars, astronomers are able to determine their distances.

Summary

When you learn of an object such as a star as being a certain number of light-years away, simply multiply that number by six trillion miles per light-year to find its distance from the sun. We can't see anything until its light reaches us. The speed of light is so fast that we see close objects almost instantaneously. However, the farther the object, the later we see it. The nearest star to our solar system is about four light-years away. That's six trillion times four or twenty-four trillion miles away from Earth. Consider these series of events. The light from this star will not be seen from Earth until four years after its light was emitted, and should this star extinguish, its light will not vanish until four years later. These scenarios can be mind-boggling especially when we consider that most stars are several billion light-years away.

Chapter 7

Thoughts from Physics

Introduction

An understanding of our physical world provides an appreciation of our existence as well as the existence of nature. We are more inclined to think about the many things that we normally take for granted. Things that are so natural they seldom cross our minds. Throughout this chapter, I have researched the physics which we are faced with on a daily basis that for many of us are so irrelevant to our lives that we may not feel a need to further explore. However, to know and think about them is a recipe for many thoughts of the good kind…the positive kind.

Air

Why do air molecules float? Aren't they being pulled to Earth's surface by gravity? Yes, they do get pulled down to Earth by gravity, but air molecules in the atmosphere move so fast they constantly bump into one another. All this bouncing around is what supports air molecules at higher altitudes, thus maintaining existence which otherwise would be pulled closer to the surface by gravitational force. It's called air pressure. The closer molecules get to each other, the more frequently they collide with each other and the higher the air pressure. However, when they get too close together, the air pressure pushes them apart. Then when they get too far apart, gravity pulls them down and closer together again. The cycle then repeats.

Bubbles rise in water?

We like to believe that since air inside a bubble is less dense than water, that air causes the bubble to rise. When in fact, the water is being pulled down by gravitational force, thus pushing the bubble upward to the surface.

Boiling Point

How does salt increase the boiling point of a liquid? Liquid boils when its vapor pressure becomes greater than the air pressure above it. Salt molecules are so weak that they weaken water molecules, causing the water molecules to struggle to get past the surface pressure and into the air molecules. Thus salt in water takes longer to boil.

Color of Snow

The number of bubbles in snow are significantly reduced whenever snow is compacted. Light that enters compacted snow travels a longer distance before it emerges and gives the red end of the color spectrum enough space to be absorbed. The light on the surface then appears blue. Compacted snow or a deep hole in snow allows photon waves to reflect back and forth except for the blue wavelengths. Therefore, we see blue within ice and snow. Blue ice is safer because it's stronger.

Craters

Since the moon has many more craters on its surface than Earth, you would think it's because the moon attracts more asteroids (meteorites) than Earth, right?

Well, Earth *does* attract many more asteroids than the moon because Earth's gravitational force is much greater than the moon's force to "pull in" celestial bodies. The reason we don't see craters on Earth's surface is because Earth possesses many features that can remove any evidence of damage to its surface caused by celestial impacts, whereby the moon does not possess such dramatic features and therefore impacts from objects falling on the moon's surface remains on its surface forever. Although the moon gets hit with fewer space material than Earth, the moon is powerless to do anything about it, and thus craters on the moon become frozen in time and remain there forever! Features on Earth which remove any evidence of craters include:

- Rocks—Earth's surface is capable of forming new rocks as well as having the capability to pulverize old rocks. Earth's surface is recycled many times over, and craters are covered up during the process.
- Weather—Earth has weather, water, vegetation, and other features which act to break apart and wear down the ground as well as rocks. Erosion also breaks craters down completely. Moon has no erosion because it has no atmosphere. Nothing on the moon can remove marks on its surface. In fact, footprints from our astronauts since 1969 are still visible on the moon!
- Lava—Volcanic lava flow covers the craters on Earth, whereas the moon has no volcanos, and therefore, craters cannot be covered up. Craters remain on the surface of the moon forever.

Evaporation

Heated water is necessary for evaporation to take place. Energy breaks the bonds with neighboring molecules, which hold water molecules together. Once broken, evaporation occurs. Then when saturated air is cooled below the dew point (the temperature of which air must be cooled to become fully saturated), such as on the outside of a glass of ice water, saturation occurs until the rate of evaporation, and the rate of condensation are equal. At this point, the relative humidity in the air is 100 percent.

Fire

When water comes in contact with fire, water turns to steam. The steam then absorbs most of the heat, thus making the burning material too cool to continue burning. Although hot water will turn to steam slightly quicker and will extinguish a fire faster than cold water, there's less than only 1 percent advantage in using hot water… food for thought!

Forces

There are four natural forces in all of nature. I have placed these forces in the order of their strengths with the first being the strongest.

- Strong nuclear forces
  This the strongest and physically smallest of the four forces in our universe. Strong forces are the force or charge that bonds electrons, neutrons, and protons of the nucleus inside an atom.
- Electromagnetic forces
  These forces are all forms of light including the sunlight, electric light bulbs, radio and television transmitting waves, microwaves, and radar.
- Weak nuclear forces
  The forces responsible for the decay of the nuclei in atoms.
- Gravitational forces
  The weakest but physically largest of the four forces in our universe are the gravitational forces, which draws all matter to the center of Earth.

Free Falling

While falling in air, an object will eventually obtain a maximum and steady velocity referred to as "terminal velocity" and will maintain that speed until reaching the ground. Terminal velocity occurs when the force of gravity pulling an object downward is balanced with the force of air resistance, pushing an object upward. The speed that an object reaches depends on its shape, size, and weight, such as a marble versus a brick, as these characteristics offer different areas of friction against the air, thereby reaching the ground at different times. It is not possible for any object to obtain a speed greater than its terminal velocity. At terminal velocity, objects feel zero acceleration, thus the term *free-falling*.

However, in a vacuum, a much different situation occurs. The concepts of terminal velocity and free-falling do not exist because of the absence of air resistance. An object falling in a vacuum will accelerate at 32.17 feet (9.89 meters) per second and for every second thereafter due to the constant pull of gravity regardless of the shape, size, or weight of the object and due to the lack of air friction. The longer an object falls in a vacuum, the faster its velocity and the greater the distance covered. Under this situation, objects dropped in a vacuum at the same time will all experience the same velocity and will all land at the same time.

Distance covered

This formula determines the distance covered by an object falling in a vacuum:

$$D = (0.5)(g)(t^2)$$

Where:

D = distance covered during falling in a vacuum

g = gravity acceleration of 32.17 feet (9.89 meters) per second, per second

t = number of seconds falling

Example: Calculate the distance covered by an object falling in a vacuum after five seconds.

$$D = (0.5)(g)(t^2)$$
$$D = (0.5)(9.89 \text{ meters per second})(\text{number of seconds falling}^2)$$
$$D = (0.5)(32.17 \text{ feet})(5 \text{ seconds}^2)$$
$$D = (0.5)(32.17 \text{ feet})(25 \text{ seconds})$$

D = 402.12 feet (0.076 miles) distance covered

Velocity

This formula determines the velocity of an object falling in a vacuum:

V = (g) (t)

Where:
V = velocity an object falling in a vacuum
g = gravity acceleration of 32.17 feet (9.8 meters) per second, per second
t = elapsed seconds falling.

After five seconds, an object falling in a vacuum will attain a velocity of 32.17 feet (9.8 meters) per second × 5 seconds = 160.85 feet (0.03 miles) per second. For every second thereafter, the speed of the object will increase by 32.17 feet per second times the number of seconds until reaching the ground.

Example: Calculate the velocity of an object after falling in a vacuum for five seconds.
V = (10 meters) (number of seconds falling)
V = (32.17 feet) (5 seconds)
V = 160.85 feet per second after 5 seconds.
0.03 miles per second after 5 seconds.
108.0 miles per hour after 5 seconds.

After ten seconds
V = (32.17 feet) (10)
V = 321.70 feet per second after 10 seconds
0.06 miles per second after 10 seconds
216 miles per hour after 10 seconds

The velocity of an object falling in a vacuum is proportional to the amount of time it falls. The longer an object falls, the greater its velocity.

Gravity

Isaac Newton felt that gravity is a force that acts between any two objects having mass. No matter what the objects are made of, both objects get pulled toward each other simply because they possess mass. However, Albert Einstein stated that riding up in an elevator provides a similar sensation to that of gravity and that acceleration and gravity are the same. Einstein further stated that no such force is required and, in fact, no such force even exists.

Einstein imagined occupying a windowless box in outer space that was accelerated to a stable rate by some unknown propulsion device. It would be impossible for anyone inside the box to tell whether they were stationary on Earth or moving in space because all experiences such as pouring a drink, juggling balls, standing up, sitting down, or weighing themselves on a scale would all be the same. Based on this thought experiment, Einstein concluded that gravity is not a force of attraction because no such force is required. Instead, gravity is something quite different. Gravity is created through a curvature in the fabric of space-time.

Fabric of space-time

Yes, as with many, I also wrestled with this concept until I began to consider the typical analogy of a trampoline. Suppose a heavy object such as a large bowling ball were placed in the center of a trampoline. Its weight would cause the center of the trampoline to sag. Now drop a golf ball on the edge of the trampoline. It would immediately roll to the center and collide with the bowling ball. Now instead of simply dropping the golf ball on the outer edge, you push it to roll around the trampoline only to discover the golf ball would travel a short distance before quickly finding its way to again collide with the bowling ball. However, if you could push the golf ball fast enough and maintain a constant acceleration, it would continue to roll around the trampoline and never collide with bowling ball. The combination of the trampoline fabric drawing the golf ball toward its center and the acceleration speed of the golf ball is believed to be much like how Earth orbits the sun.

We feel the force of gravity only because we are perched upon a surface that gives us weight. Remove that surface, and gravity would no longer feel like anything at all. We would be weightless. Earth seems to be in orbit around the sun, but in fact, Earth is going straight along a space-time surface that is curved or warped by the mass of the sun. For example, imagine driving on what appears to be a straight highway from Toronto to Montreal. The straightest route between any two cities is always curved by the surface of the Earth. In fact, if the trip were long enough, any straight-line journey along the surface of the Earth would eventually result in a circle.

Earth pulls you down while you pull Earth up. The two forces meet where your feet touch the ground, and since they are equal and opposite, you remain there. If there were only the downward force, then you'd shoot to the center of the Earth. Conversely, if there were only the upward force, you'd shoot off into space. The equal and opposite reaction is what allows us to stand on the surface of the earth as stated in Newton's third law: for every action, there is an equal and opposite reaction.

Newton said that a falling apple would be attracted to Earth due to Earth's gravitational force on the apple. But Einstein had a deeper understanding of what actually attracted the apple to Earth and explained that the apple fell to Earth via the space-time fabric created by the mass of Earth. Here's another way to think of gravity. Jump out of an airplane at fifteen thousand feet without a parachute. (No, please don't.) Now roll over to look upward. You could easily imagine yourself at rest while riding through space. There would be a stiff wind beating against you while you're at rest. The wind seems to be moving and not you. This realization that gravity and acceleration are really the same provides the central insight to Einstein's theory of general relativity.

Now roll over to look downward. Uh-oh…there's a good-sized planet rushing straight up at you. Still it's Earth that seems to be moving toward you, so it will be Earth's fault when you collide! You can try a similar experiment while standing on the ground. You would think that you are pushing down against the earth with your weight and it's your weight that keeps you from flying away, but you could just as accurately turn this perception around and imagine it is the earth that is *pushing up* against you, giving you the illusion of weight just as the floor of an upward accelerating elevator pushes up against you.

Can anyone explain "space-time" in simple terms? I don't think so. I've done a lot of research on this concept, and in paraphrasing the best explanation, I start with the question where are you right *now*? Assuming you don't know, you are in the middle of nowhere, and I must communicate your location to others. To do this, I would need several pieces of information from you:

- Your latitude
- Your longitude
- Your altitude
- Your moment in time

These coordinates will give me the three dimensions x, y, z, to your location, which we will call *space*. Now what if we removed the *now*, the three dimensions won't be enough to locate you. I could specify your location as x, y, z, but that's only where you are "now" and not where you were previously That's why we need to also specify the "time" in which you were at that location, making your actual coordinates t, x, y, z your location in four-dimensional space-time.

We normally don't consider your time in terms of space-time because the time component is either ignored or of no significance since we don't normally think about time as another coordinate like x, y, z space.

Do all objects fall at the same speed?

Aristotle claimed that heavy objects fall faster than lighter objects. However, Galileo stated the gravitational force pulling a heavy mass down is greater than the gravitational force pulling a light mass down. Since it takes more force to accelerate a heavy mass and a less force to accelerate a lighter mass, these two effects cancel each other out, resulting in both objects falling at the same speed.

This experiment was proven by astronaut David Scot on the moon during the *Apollo 15* mission in 1971. Astronaut Scot dropped a 46.5 ounce (1.32 kg) hammer and a 1.06 ounce (0.03 kg) falcon feather at the same time from about 3.5 feet, and they both landed on the moon's surface at the same time.

Galileo's proof

What if we tie a heavy object to a light object? Keep in mind that each object has its own individual mass and center of gravity. Now, by Aristotle's reasoning, during a fall, the lighter object would slow down the heavier object, and at the same time, the heavier object would speed up the lighter object, and the resulting speed of the combined light and heavy objects would be somewhere in between the speed of the two individually or an average speed. But the mass of the two combined is greater than the mass of either one, a situation which cannot exist when the two are tied. This demonstrates that the combination of both objects cannot fall slower than the faster object and, at the same time, cannot fall faster than the slower object!

Aristotle
(384 BCE to 322 BCE)

Galileo Galilei
(February 15, 1564, to January 8, 1642)

Isaac Newton
(January 4, 1643, to March 31, 1727)

Albert Einstein
(March 14, 1879, to April 18, 1955)

Greenhouse Effect

What is the greenhouse effect?

When heat from the sun reaches Earth, the surface of Earth absorbs some of the heat and radiates some back into the atmosphere as infrared waves. CO_2 in the atmosphere then reflects some of that heat back to Earth, and some pass freely back into space. This is nature's design to cause our planet's temperature to maintain a balance between how much heat is imported to our planet versus how much heat is exported from our planet. Thus the right amount of carbon dioxide gas (CO_2) is provided by nature in order to keep our Earth warm and, at the same time, prevent a constant freeze.

However, an excessive concentration of CO_2 created by human activities, such as burning fossil fuels, oil, coal, wildfires, and tree clearings, act as a blanket or a shield around our planet that traps and prevents heat from normally returning back into space. That heat is returned back to Earth to further warm our planet and thus contributing to the "greenhouse effect."

Will plants and trees absorb excess CO_2?

Yes, but these advantageous carbon dioxide eaters just cannot work fast enough to keep Mother Nature ahead of the race. Besides, most of these plants and trees store the CO_2 in their rooting systems of which are regularly visited by human invaders for burning and rebuilding. We all need to realize that global warming is real; real enough to show its devastating evidence worldwide.

Hearing

The table below provides an approximate range of frequencies that can be heard by various creatures. These ranges of frequencies are based on sound levels of approximately 60 db., which is about the typical level of humans talking.

The following table is in the range from the lowest to the highest.

Elephant	4 Hz to 12 kHz
Human	30 Hz to 20 kHz
Bird	40 Hz to 20 kHz
Groundhog	30 Hz to 30 kHz
Cat	500 Hz 40 kHz
Squirrel	113 Hz to 49 kHz
Chipmunk	20 Hz to 50 kHz
Hamster	30 Hz to 50 kHz
Dog	40 Hz to 60 kHz
Mouse	1 kHz to 70 kHz
Dolphin	20 Hz to 150 kHz
Bat	1 kHz to 200 kHz

(Hz = hertz per second; kHz = 1,000 hertz per second)

Hydrogen Bonding

Water has a relatively high boiling point due to hydrogen bonding. Since a great deal of thermal energy is required to break the bonds between water molecules, the average heat emitted by the sun is not enough to result in boiling. Hydrogen bonds ensures the reduction of temperature extremes in large bodies of water. Without hydrogen bonds, water in oceans and lakes would begin to rapidly boil due to the vast decrease in boiling point, resulting in massive problems for life on Earth.

Shadow

How much does a shadow weigh? When you cast a shadow on an object, will the weight of that object increase or decrease? In theory, the weight of the object will decrease! It turns out that the object will decrease in weight but unmeasurably. Photons, such as the sun, moon, or artificial light sources, striking an object will move atoms away from that object, thereby decreasing the weight of the object.

Sound, Sight, Feel, Taste, and Smell Don't Exist! Really?

Prior to reading this section, we need to address that there are some people who believe we hear with our ears, see with our eyes, feel with our skin, taste with our tongues, and smell with our nose. Although that belief may be more appropriate and acceptable, many believe that replacing the word "with" with the word "through" is more accurate! The entire world and everything in it comes into existence only in our brain via our ears, eyes, touch, tongue, and nose sense organs.

The information received by these senses stimulates their relative organs which are then instantly converted into electrical signals that are "pre-wired" to respective areas within our brain for analyses and processing. Only at this point will the entire world and everything in it comes into existence to us, and only then can we hear leaves rustling in the wind; see formed objects like buildings, cars, and people; feel various materials and sensations; smell roses; and taste Snicker candy bars. All still exist only within our imaginations.

Although all these activities appear real in our brains, outside of our brains they are only undistinguishable, soundless, sightless, sensationless, tasteless, and smell-less clouds of complex atoms. There cannot be any such activities within our brain; there are only electrical impulses. This is simply a scientific description of the functions of our perception. Do we actually "see" anything in the universe with our eyes? No and yes. No, because we cannot "see" anything at all! Our eyes are basically lenses that take in the electromagnetic waves (particles and photons) of which all objects are made of. And, yes, because while these electromagnetic waves are passing through our eye lenses, they become transformed into electrical pulses and sent to our brains where we simply "imagine" all objects in the universe.

Each of these sense organs deals with its own types of atoms and molecules from which they are made, causing them to react in the form of electrical pulse not in sound, sight, feel, taste, or smell but rather in streams of electrical pulses, activating neurons in the brain which then processes one stream into sound, another stream into vision, and so on. We truly live our entire lives within our brain.

This means that we experience the entire world as formed by the electric signals in our brains. All our interpretations about the world are comprised of electrical signals, and our brain is what processes these signals to become meaningful to us. Throughout our lives, many of us assume the world exists outside of us in the same way as we experience it when in fact the world lives within us inside a tiny segment of our brains. Our dreams, whether black and white or in color for example, do not actually exist anywhere in our universe at all, but instead they are created and truly do exist but only in our imagination…in our brains. How amazing is it that even during our dreams, our brains are still capable of creating the necessary senses even while our physical senses are at rest!

Even more amazing is that we "experience" emotions, sadness, happiness, laughter, hurt, fear, and anxiety in our dreams as we do when fully awake! Oh, let's not forget that our brain is always in total darkness! Yes, our brain rests in total darkness, yet we have experienced our entire life of feelings, experiences, images, colors, sounds, smells, everything that this incredible Earth has given to us and beyond. Our belief and strong faith have provided our greatest of positive thoughts in knowing that after our brain no longer functions and after we are no longer part of this Earth, take comfort that, like desert, "the best has yet to come."

Is our brain similar to our computer?

Yes, and in many ways, and I'm glad you asked because I like using a computer to illustrate the similarities of its functions to the functions of our brains. Suppose our computer lasted for a human lifetime, its electrical power source would be similar to our long-lasting beating heart. Its processor would be like our brain and its display and paper like our eyes. So then how does a computer display or print a document? The final printed document was created and processed inside the computer from individual electrical signals represented by each character typed on the keyboard, similar to the flow of electrical signals carried by our sensory organs and processed inside our brains.

The keyboard signals are then converted in the computer processor, similar to our brain, then displayed on a screen or printed on paper, similar to our eyes. You would then think it's a miracle since the computer received only a series of events (commands) via its "sensors" from the keyboard or mouse then convert these commands into electrical pulses pre-wired to the computer processor. *The computer processor reveals all the undisguisable signals from the keyboard outside of the computer while the brain reveals all the undisguisable signals from the outside world.* (Although today's technology allows computers to recognize fingerprints and facial expressions, the analogy in this section is used for the purpose of explanation).

There's nothing outside of the computer that physically represents the printed document for everything entering the computer becomes processed and then formed within the computer's processor as evidenced by colorful images on the display and colorful images on printed paper.

When we look at an object, what enters our eyes are not the objects outside of us but rather the object as they exist in our brain. We will never be able to directly see the electrons, atoms, and molecules responsible for the objects. How then can such bright and colorful objects appear in our brains? There is another explanation that should be considered. Light cannot possibly penetrate into the physical and total darkness area in which the brain is located. However, incredible as it may seem, all objects are created in the "ever dark" brain. We may observe a fire for hours, for example, but our brain never concerns itself with the light or heat from the fire. Even while we see light from the fire, or even attempt to feel its heat, still our brain remains in total darkness and at a constant temperature.

It is amazing that even in total darkness, the electrical signals are still being processed into colorful and bright visions. If we think deeply, we will be amazed by these miracles. Despite the many years of research, researchers have not been able to provide any type of vision corrections for our eyes that gives the same sharpness and high quality as what the brain is able to produce.

Electromagnet waves, or light as we may call it, is a form of energy which comes into existence only after passing through the lenses of the eyes of a person and most creatures. Since our existence, there has never been any light outside of our bodies. When photons reach our eyes, we see the colorful, bright, and light-filled world. However, there isn't one single color that exists in the entire universe. Colors are formed only in our brains. Outside our eyes colors are only electromagnetic waves (photons) with different amplitudes and different frequencies within our visual color spectrum.

The sun emits an amazing wide range of electromagnetic waves (radiation). However, our brains are only capable of receiving and processing a very small segment from 400 THz to 750 THz of the entire spectrum. (THz stands for terahertz or 1 trillion hertz or 1 trillion cycles per second). The waves that are seen in our brains as red are located within the frequency range of 400 to 480 THz, orange in the range of 480 to 510 THz, yellow from 510 to 530 THz, green from 530 to 600 THz, blue from 600 to 670 THz, indigo from 670 to 700 THz, and violet from the frequency range of 700 to 750 THz.

The lower frequencies around 400 THz are typically referred to as "photons" while the upper frequencies around 750 THz are typically referred to as "particles."

What reaches our brains is the energy from those waves. Only when our brains interpret and process this energy, by measuring the different frequencies of waves, can we then see colors. The car is not blue, the evergreen trees are not green, bananas are not yellow, and cherries are not red. They appear in those colors because of the way we perceive them within our brains. The photons from the sun or from any other form of light within our visible color spectrum reflect an object into our eyes in varying frequencies respective to the object.

Color blindness, for example, confirms that colors are formed in our brains. A person with color blindness is unable to differentiate between red and green colors not because the photons have somehow changed only for that color-blinded individual but rather because of the processing differences within that individual's brain. All the qualities of colorful objects that we may think exists and belong to the outside world only exist and belong in our brains. If the same things can be red and spicy for some people but not for others, this simply suggests that "things" must, therefore, only exist in our brains.

Can sound travel through space?

No. Since sound needs air molecules to carry its vibration, it can't travel through the vacuum of space. If we were to watch two spaceships collide into each other, we would not hear the explosion unless we were in one of the spaceships. The impact would cause the air molecules inside the ship to compress against our ears, which would then trigger the electrical pulses pre-wired to our brains and produce the "sound." Space, as well as on the moon, have no atmosphere. Astronauts in space or on the surface of the moon communicate among each other and with their command center on Earth via electromagnetic waves which they transmit and receive from their radio transmitters and receivers.

Do audio frequencies have sound such as those frequencies created from slamming a car door? No. Slamming a car door only causes its surrounding air molecules to compress and move within various frequencies. Humans will hear in the range from 40 Hz to 20,000 Hz. Sound is not produced but rather air molecules are moved, which enters our ears where transformation to audible sounds then occurs.

Humans and most creatures hear sounds via compressed air molecules that enter our inner ears, vibrates our audio ear bones, creates electrical pulses, and sends them to our brain. It's only at this point are we able to "hear" the effects of the door slamming. Sound exists only within our brains and not from outside our bodies. Yes, everything around us may appear to exist but only in very complex clouds of atoms within the electromagnetic waves spectrum in the universe, which we eventually interpret, and all the compressed air molecules for the sounds we eventually interpret. For it's through our miraculous senses and brains that we can interpret and create what "they seem to be."

Surely, we can now see beyond our race, religion, political beliefs, our color, faults, sexual orientations, and our gender and fully appreciate the many miracles given to each of us. During the last few chapters, we referred to miracles. Miracles that not only occur within every human and most creatures every second or every moment but in fact are also occurring on an ongoing, uninterrupted, and continual basis. The text that we are currently reading, for example, is being created and only exist within our brains.

In conclusion, any object in our universe, such as a tree is not a tree. It is, however, an undisguisable "cloud" of complex atoms that is formed by our Creator and by our environment in such a way that it becomes a tree only within our brain…our imagination. Our color, our race, our choice of religious beliefs, sexual orientation, or our feelings toward one another does not affect or should it ever influence this very special once-in-a-lifetime gift we all possess.

Weightlessness

Astronauts aboard the orbiting International Space Station appear to be weightless. In fact, they *are* weightless but not because they have escaped beyond the reach of Earth's gravity. Instead, the astronauts and their space station are in a state of free fall toward Earth. They avoid striking planet Earth for the same reason Earth doesn't crash into the sun: because they are moving very fast and the space station speed is just enough to prevent colliding with Earth.

Although it might not seem like it, Earth is falling into the even deeper hollow in space-time caused by the mass of the sun. The only thing preventing a collision with the sun is Earth's velocity, which is just enough to ensure that in its never-ending downward spiral toward the sun is much like the spaceship which keeps missing Earth. This constant state of free fall, coupled with an appropriate velocity, is what constitutes an orbit. But the important point for relativity theory is that space-time is curved by mass. A star, planet, or any mass warps space and time.

Think of a daredevil balancing on a tightrope strung across the Niagara Falls. From an observer's perspective, the daredevil walks from one end of the falls straight to his destination on the other end of the falls, just as you may think that you can drive straight from Toronto to Montreal. This is an illusion. In fact, if you plot the daredevil's progress from the same horizontal plane, you will see that the acrobat's tightrope sags significantly as he is drawn into the hollow in space-time caused by the mass of the Earth. His journey is curved. We are all drawn into that same hollow, and this explains why we don't drift away into space. In effect, we are all in the act of falling toward the center of the Earth, and we would if only Earth's surface didn't get in the way.

A spaceship, and everything inside it, is moving fast enough that as it falls toward the Earth, the surface of the Earth curves away from it. The spaceship is always falling toward the Earth, but it never gets there. Much like the airplane that's set to a specified altitude and thrusting forward. The airplane will not fall to Earth but instead will arc around the Earth while maintaining its preset altitude. If you were six feet tall, standing on a perfectly flat and level 5 mile stretch of a highway, you would be able to see a flashlight lying perfectly flat on the level highway at approximately 3.0 miles away. But if the flashlight were to be moved farther back to say 3.1 miles away from you, you would no longer be able to see its light.

Earth's curvature is what actually makes astronauts weightless in space. With a forward motion of five miles per second, astronauts are falling toward the Earth at the same rate that the curvature of the Earth is falling away from them. They are actually in a state of free fall. Einstein explained that it's no different than falling while in an elevator. The bottom of the elevator is moving away from you at the same rate at which you are falling. You are falling, but you just never hit anything.

Chapter 8

Thoughts from How It Works

Introduction

Many of us are curious about how things work. It seems to put some good thoughts in our minds after acquiring some understanding and at the same time leaving little to no room for any negative thoughts. Many positive thoughts have come from learning about how things work. Being curious and following up with the learning stage is fascinating. Today we have all the tools and technology we need to quickly learn about how things work while years ago we had to walk to the library and spend hours going through many books, not to mention note writing. I have included this chapter to enhance our thought experiences.

Air Conditioner

Sizing room air conditioners

Central air conditioners are rated in "tons," nothing to do with weight, but derived from the fact that it takes 288,000 Btus (British thermal units, a unit of heat) to melt a one-ton block of ice in a twenty-four-hour period. Therefore, 288,000/24 hours = 12,000 Btus per hour. However, room air conditioners are rated in Btu. For each additional person in a room, add 600 Btus. If the room air conditioner is used in a kitchen, increase the Btu capacity by 4,000 Btus. If the room is sunny, increase the Btu capacity by 10 percent. If the room is shaded, reduce the Btu capacity by 10 percent. Rule of thumb…20 Btus per room square foot area.

Square Foot Area (Approx.)	A/C Btu (Approx.)
450 to 700	10,000 to 12,000
700 to 1,000	12,000 to 18,000
1,000 to 1,500	18,000 to 24,000
1,500 to 2,000	24,000 to 30,000

Black Tires?

Why black? Blue tires would match my car! Tires are black because a key ingredient, carbon black, is added to the mix of natural and synthetic rubber. Carbon black are tiny dustlike particles that act like a bonding agent for the other ingredients used within the tire. Carbon black has the added feature of dissipating heat of the sun, thus protecting the tire against ozone and UV damage.

No other additive has been found to be as effective as carbon black at protecting the rubber and prolonging the life of tires. In the absence of carbon black, ozone and UV rays would otherwise attack the molecules and chemical bonds of the rubber, which over time would cause the rubber to deteriorate and weaken.

Center of the USA

There are two states that claim to being located in the center of the United States. The precise geographical north, south, east, and west center of the United States is Rugby, North Dakota. Another center in the lower forty-eight states is located north of Lebanon, Kansas, or approximately twelve miles south of the border between Kansas and Nebraska. This was determined by finding the center of gravity or the point at which the United States map would balance if it were of uniform thickness. I tend to favor no. 1.

Cloud Altitude

Have you ever looked at a cloud and wondered how high it was? You may have estimated three hundred feet? Eight hundred feet? Well, you can use the following formula to estimate cloud altitude. However, this method is only approximate as there are many variables, such as humidity, wind, cloud types, and cloud formations, which affect the accuracy.

The difference between surface air temperature and dew point is called the "spread." Divide the spread by 4.4 if temperatures used are in degrees Fahrenheit (or divide by 2.5 if temperatures used are in degrees Celsius). Then multiply the result by one thousand to give the altitude of the cloud base in feet above ground.

Formula

$Ch = (S / 4.4) (1,000)$
Where:
Ch = Cloud height
S = Deference between the dew point and the air temperature

Example 1

Suppose the air temperature is 60°F and the dew point is 40°F
$Ch = (S / 4.4) (1,000)$
$Ch = [(60-40) / 4.4) (1,000)]$
$Ch = [(20 / 4.4) (1,000)]$
$Ch = (4.5) (1,000)$
$Ch = 4,500$ feet

Example 2

Suppose the air temperature is 90°F and the dew point is 15°F
$Ch = (S / 4.4) (1,000)$
$Ch = [(90-15) /4.4) (1,000)]$
$Ch = [(75 / 4.4) (1,000)]$

Ch = (17) (1,000)
Ch = 17,000 feet

Continents

The number of continents, their locations, and their descriptions have never been agreed upon. However, the seven continents in this chapter have been generally accepted. Ignoring north and south prefixes, the first and last letters of all accepted seven continent names on the planet are the same.

- AsiA
- AfricA
- AmericA (North)
- AmericA (South)
- AntarcticA
- EuropE
- AustraliA

Chopsticks

How to use chopsticks. Originated in China, chopsticks are a sign of attitude of the educated against warrior swords. Chopsticks were, therefore, favored over silverware for eating.

Japanese chopsticks are made of bamboo wood and are pointed. Chinese chopsticks are also made of wood but are blunt. South Korean chopsticks are flat and made of stainless steel.

To use chopsticks, do the following:

1. Palm up, place the center of chopstick no. 1 under the inside web of the thumb and on the tip of the fourth ring finger.
2. Grip the center of chopstick no. 2 with the thumb tip, first fingertip, and second fingertip.
3. Make chopstick tips even.

4. To pick up food, raise the tip of chopstick no. 2 for an opening for food.
5. Lower chopstick no. 2 to firmly clamp the food between chopsticks no. 1 and no. 2.
6. Chopstick no. 2 moves while the bottom of chopstick no. 1 remains stationary.
7. Use the opposite end of the chopsticks to move food from a shared bowl to your plate.

Clothes Iron

The heat and weight of the clothes iron loosens the ties between long chains of molecules that exist in polymer fiber materials. The fibers are stretched, and the fabric maintains its new shape when cooled. Some materials, such as cotton, require the use of water to loosen the intermolecular bonds. Many materials developed in the twentieth century need little to no ironing.

Compass

The concept behind using a compass to find your destination is quite simple. Since the "North" end of the pointing needle always points to north, simply point the "direction of travel" arrow to your destination then rotate the bezel and position the double arrow (lubber line) over the north-pointing needle. Now all you need to do is walk in the direction of your direction arrow while keeping the lubber line over north until you reach your destination. However, as you slightly drift away from your destination, the magnetic north-pointing needle will also drift away from the lubber line.

This means you are off course, and you will need to change your direction to cause the north-pointing needle to move back inside the lubber line.

How many of us know how to use a typical compass to find our way home or to find our way back to our camp sites? We may have learned how to use a compass while in the Boy Scouts or Girl Scouts, but for those who were never in the scouts, here's the way I set up and use my compass.

Setting the compass

I place an official trail chart or map on a flat surface and identify my starting point and location to my final destination. I turn the chart so that north faces upward then place the compass on the starting point with the "direction of travel" arrow pointing toward the destination. I the rotate the compass bezel ring until the lubber line is over the "North" point of the needle. The compass is now set to use, and no further adjustments will be necessary.

During hiking, I simply turn as necessary so that the lubber line is kept inside the North needle as I walk in the direction of the direction arrow. Now during my hike, I may turn left or right as necessary but keep the direction of travel arrow straight toward my destination while maintaining the lubber line over the North needle. Following these steps takes me to my destination.

Continental Divide

The purpose of a continental divide is to flow water to either the Pacific Ocean or to the Atlantic Ocean. Rain and melted snow on the eastern sides of the continental divide drains and flows toward the Atlantic Ocean while on the western sides drains and flows toward the Pacific Ocean. Except for Antarctica, every continent has a continental divide. The continental divide or "great divide" follows mountain ranges starting in Alaska and ending at the southern tip of South America. There are some rivers that empty into the deserts and the Gulf of Mexico which never flow to the oceans.

Counterfeit Bills

Several years ago, I received a counterfeit $20 bill donated from a dear friend. I was collecting money from my musical family for a very worthy cause. When I attempted to deposit the money, the bank teller informed me that there was a counterfeit $20 among the collection. It turned out that my friend was paid that $20 bill among other legitimate denominations for a musical performance he had given that week. The bank retained the counterfeit bill, and I had to fill out several forms.

How can we tell if a United States currency is counterfeit or not? Here are some helpful guidelines:

Denom-ination	Hold to the Light, and Look for This
$1	• n/a
$50	• A watermark 5 is centered on far-right side. • Vertical line of small 5s on right of Lincoln.
$10	• A duplicate of Hamilton's watermark face is centered on the right side. • Vertical line of small 10s on the right of Hamilton.
$20	• A duplicate of Jackson's watermark face is on the lower-right corner. • Bottom-right corner shows "20" in a copper color then turns green when the top of the bill is tilted backward.
$50	• A duplicate of Grant's watermark face is centered on the right side. • Bottom right corner shows "50" in a copper color then turns green when the top of the bill is tilted backward. • Vertical line of small 50s in the center.
$100	• A duplicate of Franklin's watermark face is centered on the right side. • Bottom-right corner shows "100" in a copper color then turns green when the top of the bill is tilted backward.

How Far Can We See?

Well, there's a very simple formula to determine how far we can see. Suppose you are on the very top of a lighthouse that is one hundred feet above sea level. Looking out over the water, you can only see as far as the horizon; you cannot see beyond the curvature of the Earth. However, in order to see beyond the horizon, we need to be at a higher elevation, but regardless of our height, we can never see beyond the curvature of the Earth.

The simple formula to determine how far we can see is the square root of our height times 1.23. The "1.23" is a constant based on an arc of the circumference of the Earth. So the square root of a one-hundred-foot lighthouse is 10 × 1.23 gives the distance of 12.3 nautical miles.

Conversely, the same holds true for a ship out at sea. The purpose of its crow's nest is to increase elevation of the ship to see farther. The same formula is used to determine the distance that the crow's nest can see. So then how far is it from the top of the one-hundred-foot lighthouse to the top of a one-hundred-foot crow's nest? Use the same formula for the lighthouse (12.3 nm) and for the crow's nest (12.3 nm) and simply add the two together to give 24.6 nautical miles from the top of the lighthouse to the top of the crow's nest.

Emergency Clock

What can I use for an emergency clock?

There are three different methods which I like use to determine local time when in a situation where a clock is not available.

Method 1. This is neat! We're going to use a compass to tell the approximate local time during the daytime. I preformed this observation on May 11, 2023, at 8:30 AM (EDT). Step far away from any metallic objects. Hold the compass horizontally and in front of you with the direction of travel arrow (black double-lined arrow) on the plastic base in the direction toward the sun as in the photo below. Normally, this arrow is used for pointing to the direction of travel.

Rotate the outer bezel ring to place the lubber line (red double-lined arrow inside the compass) directly over the north-pointing magnetic needle. Rotate the degree scale on the bezel counterclockwise fifteen degrees to compensate for magnetic variation. Doing this assures proper setting to geographical true north. No further adjustments are needed.

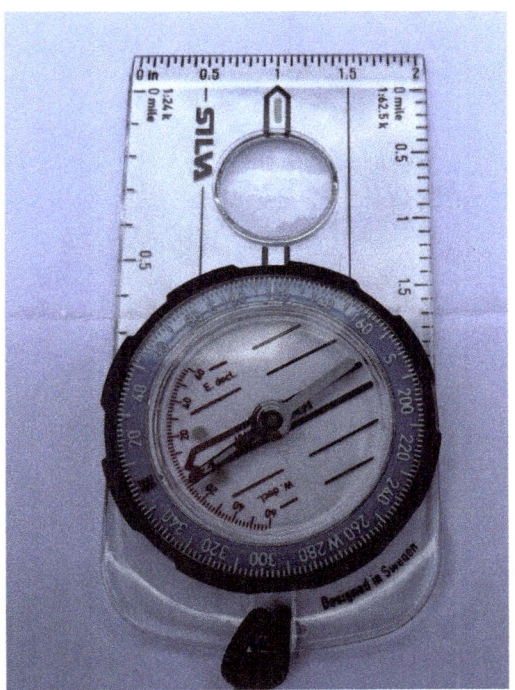

Position of the lubber line after compensating for variation
(Photo by the author)

Now flip the compass over with the direction of travel arrow facing toward you as in the photo below. Read the lubber line as a clock hour hand and use the bezel as a clock (without the clock numbers). You may need to interpolate between the hours to determine minutes.

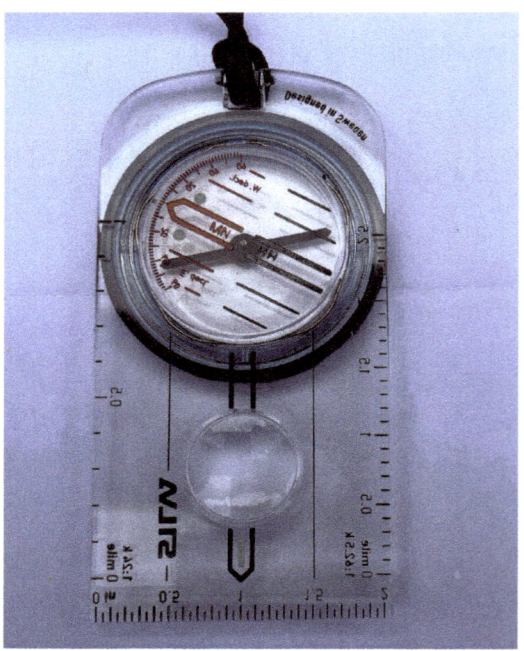

The lubber line reads about 9:30 AM
(Photo by the author)

If standard time is in effect, read the time directly as 9:30 AM. If daylight time is in effect, subtract one hour to 8:30 AM. Note that Earth rotates around its axis through the geographical north and south poles and not around magnetic north and south. The difference between the geographical poles and the magnet poles is called "variation" and is due to the ongoing gradual shifting of the magnetic properties within the core of the Earth. Magnetic north, for example, is currently at about fifteen degrees west of the geographical (true) north. Therefore, after taking your compass (magnetic) bearing to the sun, you'll need to rotate the bezel counterclockwise an additional fifteen degrees to compensate for variation as explained above. After you flip the compass over, observe the lubber line to read your approximate local standard time. Subtract one hour if on daylight time.

Your hand can tell time!

Method 2. Here's another neat way to find the time during the day without having to use anything except the fingers of your hand. I use this method frequently and find it to be accurate within fifteen to thirty minutes. It works very well on both sunny days and on not so sunny days as long as you can see the image of the sun through the clouds. Unless you are at the equator, you will need to know the time and the location on the horizon where the sun typically sets for that time of season for your latitude. The sun moves across the sky from sunrise to sunset about fifteen degrees every hour (360 degrees divided by 24 hours…of course, the sun is stationary while the earth rotates). You can tell how long it will take for the sun to set at the horizon by measuring its distance to the horizon.

Extend your arm straight outward toward the sun. Now, with outstretched little and index fingers, count the number of widths from the sun to the horizon. A child's arm, fingers, and extended arm are all relative and will provide similar results. The width between little and index fingers covers about fifteen degrees of the sky, so the amount of moves from the sun to the horizon will, therefore, give the current time. Starting at the right ride of the sun, move the width away from the sun, one width at a time, toward the horizon and count the number of moves. Subtract the number of moves from the time the sun normally sets, and that will give your current time. For example, suppose you counted 2.5 moves to the horizon and suppose the sun normally sets at 8:00 PM, here's how you can get the time: 8:00 PM - 2.5 moves to the horizon = the current time of 5:30 PM.

If you end up with half of a palm, that will represent half hour, and 1/4 of a palm will represent fifteen minutes. Be careful not to look directly into the sun at any time, especially during the first few palm moves. I always refrain from relying on my wristwatch since I find this method not only fun but also relatively accurate. Remember that the sun and Earth only recognize standard times, so be sure to compensate for daylight time.

Test your four fingers

Since the width of four fingers is similar to the width of a fist, we will use the fist in this exercise. Make fists with both hands and label the fists "fist A" and "fist B." Extend one arm outward from your side. Position fist A horizontally and level to the horizon, with the little finger side of the fist facing downward and the thumb side facing upward. Place fist B on top of fist A then alternate fists until both arms are directly overhead. The fist count should be nine. Nine fists × 10 degrees per fist = 90 degrees or the angle from the horizon to your overhead zenith. I have listed a guide for using the hand to determine the approximate distances in degrees between celestial objects in the sky, with arm stretched outward to the sky:

1 degree = the width of the little fingertip
5 degrees = the width of the three middle fingers
10 degrees = the width of a fist
15 degrees = the width of stretched out little and index fingers
20 degrees = the width of stretched out thumb and little finger

The stars can tell time

Method 3. This method allows us to determine our local time during the nighttime by observing the Big Dipper and the North Star (Polaris). They form a giant twenty-four-hour analog clock in the sky. The Big Dipper is part of the Ursa Major Great Bear constellation. However, the Big Dipper stars are commonly used to help locate Polaris. To find the Big Dipper, look for a three-star pot handle connected to a four-star square bowl (see sketch below).

Draw an imaginary line through the two bowl stars of the Big Dipper (the two stars farthest from its handle) to Polaris. The length to Polaris will be approximately five times the distance between the two outer bowl stars. This line will be the hour hand. The imaginary clock numbers remain stationary and cover a twenty-four-hour period while the hour hand of the Big Dipper moves counterclockwise. To use the sky clock, locate the Big Dipper then locate its bowl.

Draw an imaginary line to Polaris and determine the sky clock time. In this scenario, let's suppose the sky clock reads 10:30 PM. Now we need to make a correction factor to correct for calendar variations. If the current month is not March 6, we need to figure the number of months from March 6 then multiply that number by 2 then subtract the product from 10:30 PM to get your actual time. Note that the number of months from March 6 is an adjustment factor for the orbital period of moon vs. Earth.

   If the current month is close to the sixth, then simply count the number of months from March 6. However, if the current month is the twenty-fifth, for example, then figure the fractional month by dividing 25 by 30 to give 0.8 of a month in this example. So if the current month is June 25, the number of months away from March 6 would be 3.8 months. Supposed the current date is November 25; that's about 8.8 months away from March 6. So 8.8 × 2 equals 17.6. Therefore, 10:30 PM minus 17.6 equals 5:00 PM. What will your watch read when the sky clock reads 2:00 PM on December 5?

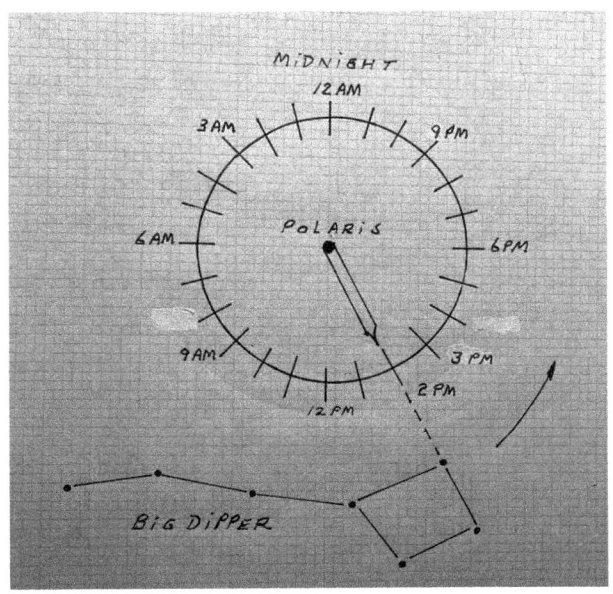

The "sky clock"
(Photo by the author)

Your time = sky clock time - (2 × number of months after March 6)
Your time = 2:00 PM − (2 × 9)
Your time = 2:00 PM − 18
Your time = 8:00 PM standard time

Of course, the stars don't actually rotate around the North Star, but they appear to do so. It's Earth's rotation which causes this effect. Here's an analogy to explain this phenomenon: suppose you were to sit on a swivel chair in the center of your living room directly under the ceiling light, which will represent the North Star, and the four walls around you were saturated with many little dots representing stars. Now you were to use your feet to rotate your chair around in one spot. The dots on the walls would appear to rotate around the stationary ceiling light.

Remember that the sun and Earth recognize only standard times, so be sure to compensate for daylight time when applicable. Simple quiz: Suppose the current month is August and the sky clock time reads 9:00 AM, can you find your actual time? If you came up with 11:00 PM standard time, you're right.

The reason the Big Dipper appears to be in different locations during different seasons and while Polaris appears to remain fixed is because Polaris is about 430 light-years away from Earth while the Big Dipper is only about 80 light-years. So depending on the season, the Big Dipper will appear anywhere from close to the horizon to overhead while the North Star remains fixed. In fact, Polaris is used in navigation to determine latitude regardless of seasons.

Emergency Compass

Introduction

Finding cardinal directions could someday come in very handy or even save a life should we ever become lost. In this neat section, we will use an analog wristwatch to demonstrate how to find the direction to south, and once we find south, the remaining cardinal directions to north, east, and west will simply be apparent. We will need part or full sunshine and an analog watch. Although most of us wear digital watches, I always keep an analog wristwatch handy in my backpack and always make sure to set the time before venturing off to unfamiliar trails.

How can we find any direction?

Be sure your analog watch is kept horizontal at all times. Now in the northern hemisphere, rotate the watch until the hour hand is in line with the direction to the sun. If the sun is too bright, line up the hour hand with a straight shadow. Now draw an imaginary line from the tip of the hour hand to the twelve o'clock mark. At the center of this line, draw another imaginary line perpendicular, and it will point to south, with the opposite direction being north.

The moon knows directions!

Another interesting way to tell directions at night is to observe the moon. After the full moon phase passes, observe any of the subsequent minor moon phases that occur anywhere between the full moon and the new moon phases. If the brightness part of the moon is on your left side, draw an imaginary line from the top to the bottom of the moon's brightness area. Draw another line perpendicular and outward from the brightness area. This line will point to the east toward sunrise. The remaining north and south directions can easily be determined.

If the bright part of the moon is on your right side, the perpendicular line will point to the east toward sunrise. Note that this exercise does not apply to the new moon phase because it cannot be seen during daytime or does it apply to the full moon phase because of its total brightness. However, while viewing a full moon phase at night, the left side will point to the east while the right side will point to the west. The same situation holds true for the daytime new moon phase. Left of the sun points to the east while the right side points to the west.

Summary

From the northern hemisphere, and while facing south toward the equator, all moon phases between the full moon and the new moon that appear bright on your left side face toward sunrise and point to east. All moon phases between the new moon and the full moon that appear bright on your right side face toward sunset and point to the west. In short, any moon that is bright on your left points to the east while any moon that is bright on your right points west. (Note that all directions are reversed if in the southern hemisphere.)

Lateral Meridian Lines

Lines of latitude are easy to understand. They run east and west on planet Earth and are evenly spaced with one another from the equator to the north and south geographical poles. Each lateral line represents ten degrees, resulting in ninety degrees from the equator to the north pole and ninety degrees from the equator to the south pole. Since the circumference around the north and south poles is about 24,900 miles, the distance from pole to pole is about 12,450 miles, the distance between the equator to each pole is about 6,225 miles. The distance between each lateral line is, therefore, about sixty-nine miles apart (6,225 ÷ 90 degrees = 69 miles).

Longitudinal Meridian Lines

On October 1851, Greenwich, England, was selected by twenty-five nations at a meeting in Washington, DC, to be the zero-degree prime meridian line as the world standard to represent the starting point for all longitudinal lines on planet Earth. The zero-degree longitudinal line runs from the geographical North Pole to the South Pole, passing directly through Greenwich, England. There are twelve longitudinal lines running east of the zero longitude and twelve longitudinal lines running west of zero longitude, totaling to twenty-four longitudinal lines. The distance between each longitudinal line represents fifteen degrees. Therefore, 15 degrees between longitudinal

246

lines times 24 lines equals 360 degrees. Since Earth takes twenty-four hours to complete one rotation, each fifteen degrees of rotation represents one hour. All longitudinal lines from the equator converge at each of the poles. The distance between the lines at the equator are, therefore, the greatest while the distances gradually reduce and become zero at each of the poles. Note that fifteen degrees for every hour translates to one degree for every four minutes.

Solar noon

As Earth rotates, we see the sun rise in the east then transits overhead from east to west at about noon then set in the west. The time when the sun transits overhead and positioned exactly between its east to west path is known as the "solar noon" and typically referred to as being "highest in the sky." This traditional description compares the distance from sunrise to the horizon and the distance from sunset to the horizon as both being the lowest distance as opposed to when the sun is at its "highest" distance when overhead.

However, I prefer to describe solar noon as the exact time when the sun transits from east to west and is positioned exactly at zenith (directly overhead) at which time the sun appears its lowest distance from Earth to overhead.

How can we find our solar noon?

The key to finding our local degree of longitude anywhere on the planet, or our solar noon, is quite simple. First, we will need a wristwatch or a clock preset to Greenwich Mean Time (GMT) so we can tell the time when the sun is over the zero-longitude line, typically about twelve noon in Greenwich, England. Greenwich Mean Time (GMT) is also known as Universal Time Coordinated, "UTC Time" or "Zulu Time"; the military and ham radio phonetic for Z represents GMT zero longitude. Take caution when setting your clock to GMT. Greenwich Mean Time is *not* adjusted for daylight time, so if you have difficulty finding GMT, use London standard time with caution. If London is on daylight time, from the last Sunday in March to the last Sunday in October, during those periods, you will need to subtract one hour.

Second, we will need a method to determine our solar noon. To find the moment of our local solar noon, let's build a solar noon locator. You may have done some research on how to build such a device only to discover that the instructions also came with complicated explanations and formulas. However, I have developed a very simple device which I hope my readers will build and enjoy.

The materials needed are the following:

- 3/4 inch thick by 12 inches by 12 inches square board (1×12×12).
- Four small 1/4-inch soft plastic adhesive tips for under each corner of the board for stability, but C-clamps will also work.
- Aluminum or steel rod 1/8-inch diameter by 6 inches long. Slightly file around one end of the rod to be sure it's square to the rod. Be careful not to file to a point, otherwise the shadows will be blurry.
- 12-inch clear plastic ruler with a 1/8-inch hole drilled near the zero-inch end of the ruler. This ruler will be used in conjunction with the above rod.
- 2-inch plastic electrical cable clamp.

Construction. I drilled a 1/8-inch diameter hole through the top center of the electrical cable clamp and another 1/8-inch diameter hole through the board centered about ½-inch from one edge of the board. I placed the board on a flat and level workbench then held the clamp over the hole on the board. I inserted the rod through the hole in the clamp and into the hole in the board. Then while holding the rod plumb, I marked the two mounting holes for the clamp then secured the clamp to the board with two screws. Finally, I taped an 8-inch by 11 1/2-inch sheet of white paper to the board. Now place the board on an outside level table. Face the board so that the shadows will fall northerly.

Note that the shadow lengths cast by the rod will vary according to the seasons. Longer days give short shadows while shorter days give long shadows. Therefore, you will find that during late fall through early spring on both sides of the winter solstice around December 21 provides the longest shadow lengths resulting in the highest accuracies. The photo below shows the solar noon locator that I constructed several years prior to writing this book.

Author's solar noon locator showing paper on
the board, ruler, rod, and clamp
(Photo by the author)

Using the solar noon locator

On a sunny and cloudless day, place the solar noon board outside on a solid and level table. Make sure the board is steady on the table. Insert the rod through the clamp, through the hole in the ruler, then in the hole in the board. Set the board so the rod faces south in order to cast north shadows on the board. It is of no concern as to which direction the board faces as long as the shadows fall on the paper.

Then about thirty minutes or so before the sun is overhead, use a sharp pencil to make a dot and write the GMT on the paper at the tip of the rod shadow. Continue making dots and writing GMT in a similar manner at every five-minute interval thereafter. Then well after the sun has passed overhead and the shadows again appear longer, swivel the ruler and measure the length to each dot to find the dot representing the shortest shadow length. The time associated with that dot represents local solar noon.

Now suppose the time read 4:40 PM GMT, this means that it took four hours and forty minutes of Earth's rotation for the solar noon to travel from the zero-longitude line in Greenwich to my solar noon time on Cape Cod. I now had the necessary GMT to find my degree of longitude after performing the following calculations:

My degree of longitude = the GMT that it took solar noon to travel from Greenwich to my solar noon times fifteen degrees per hour.

My degree of longitude = (4 hours, 40 minutes) (15 degrees per hour)

Convert 40 minutes to fractional hours by dividing 40 minutes by 60 (40/60 = 0.666 hours).

My degree of longitude = (4.66 hours) (15 degrees per hour)

My degree of longitude = 69.99 degrees

Not bad considering my actual longitude is seventy degrees!

The solar noon locator will determine your solar noon regardless of your location. However, note that the shadow lengths about one month before and one month after summer solstice will be the shortest, making the dots between shadow time intervals too close together, too difficult to read, and hence decreases accuracy.

East or west longitude?

Should the GMT clock read 9:00 AM, for example, that would mean solar noon at Greenwich occurred twenty-one hours from solar noon. Multiply 21 hours by 15 degrees per hour to give 315 degrees. Now if this figure is greater than 180 degrees, subtract 180 degrees because of the IDL. Therefore, 315 degrees - 180 degrees = 135 degrees east longitude.

How many miles between longitude lines?

Have you ever wondered what the distance is between longitudinal lines especially since the distance between these lines becomes less and less as they converge at the poles? The distances between longitudinal degrees at the equator is a simple calculation since the circumference around the equator is about 24,901.461 miles; we simply divide 24,901.461 by 360 degrees.

Here's the formula:

Miles between longitudinal degrees at the equator = Earth's circumference / 360 degrees

Miles between longitudinal degrees at the equator = 24,901.461 miles / 360 degrees

Miles between longitudinal degrees at the equator = 69.17 between longitudinal lines at equator

The distance between longitudinal lines that are above and below the equator are a little more difficult to calculate. The distance between longitude lines depends on the latitude at which they intersect. At thirty-eight degrees latitude, for example, distance between longitudinal lines equals 819 miles. At one-degree latitude, the distance is 54.6 miles. To calculate the distances between longitudinal lines at any latitude, take the cosine of the specific latitude degree then multiply by 60.

For example:

Distance between longitudinal lines at 10 degrees latitude = cos of 10 degrees × 60

Distance between longitudinal lines at 10 degrees latitude = 0.98 × 60

Distance between longitudinal lines at 10 degrees latitude = 58.8 nautical miles

Nautical Miles vs. Statute Miles

Why do navigational charts use nautical miles?

There is a very good reason navigational charts use nautical miles and not statute miles. It is because 1 nautical mile is 1/60th of a degree of latitude on navigational charts, and this makes distance calculations very easy for the mariner. Navigators can measure the distance with dividers and then simply place the divider on the lines of latitude to determine distance.

How were nautical miles determined?

As discussed earlier, lateral lines from the equator to the geographical poles are each sixty-nine miles apart. These distances are over land and referred to as statute miles. Now sixty-nine statute miles per degree is fine for driving over land but very cumbersome for navigators when working with navigational charts, especially when dealing with fractions of an hour or fractions of a degree. The number 60 as in our clock system is more convenient because equals 60 nautical miles could equal 1 lateral degree, 1 nautical mile could equal 1 minute of a degree, and 1 lateral second could equal 100 feet. To convert 69 to 60, divide 69 by 60 equals 1.15; thus the conversion factor from nautical miles to statue miles.

Example 1:

Nautical miles × 1.15 = statue miles
60 nm × 1.5 = 69 statute miles

Example 2:

Statue miles / 1.15 = nautical miles
69 / 1.15 = 60 nautical miles

Summary

Although our entire solar system, including our sun, moves within our Milky Way galaxy, the movement of the sun, however, remains constant relative to Earth. The sun neither rises nor sets. It's Earth's rotation that causes these effects. (Like an automobile GPS, your car remains stationary while the map moves.)

During Earth's rotation of 360 degrees, solar noon sunrays scan across the entire planet, covering every location from pole to pole and relative to the GMT. And since solar noon is constantly sweeping across longitudinal lines at 1/4 degree per minute while synchronized with zero degrees longitude in Greenwich, our local solar noon will accurately render our degree of longitude.

The concept of Earth rotating under the sun and causing a sweeping west to east transit of solar noon across every longitudinal line on the planet is like the analogy of Earth rotating under a giant windshield wiper blade extending from geographical pole to pole. Now envision the full length of the windshield wiper blade as being totally laser-lit from pole to pole, representing a longitudinal line. This concept is perhaps best described by placing a globe of planet Earth on a table and placing the laser-lit blade above the zero longitude line in Greenwich, representing the rays of the sun. Now holding the blade constant, rotate the globe slowly counterclockwise (looking down from the geographical North Pole) at 1/4 degree per minute (difficult to impossible!). During Earth's rotation, every location under the laser-lit blade will experience its light first approaching from sunrise, then directly overhead, then passing to sunset.

In the northern hemisphere, "approaching" will be from the east. "Directly overhead" will be solar noon, and "passing" will be to the west. All this occurs while the blade (sun) is stationary and Earth is rotating. The blade covered wide distances between the longitudinal lines at the equator while simultaneously covering narrow distances between longitudinal lines approaching both poles. Although the distance between longitudinal lines at the equator are greater, the speed of Earth's rotation is faster. And although the distances between longitudinal lines approaching the poles become much smaller, the speed of Earth's rotation is slower. This phenomenon is explained by the differences of Earth's circumferences at the equator versus the differences of Earth's circumferences approaching the poles and further describes the blade (or the sun) as being stationary while Earth rotates.

Fire Hydrants

Did you ever wonder why fire hydrants are painted in different colors? The colors of a fire hydrant provide the fire department with information about the water from the hydrant and about its location around the area. The barrel (body) color of fire hydrants reveals the method by which the water is supplied to the hydrant. The outlet (side plugs) colors tell the amount of water pressure in pounds per square inch. The color of the bonnet (top cap) tells the water flow in gallons per minute.

Although there are no laws governing fire hydrant color coding, there are, however, guidelines in which towns may or may not follow. The intent of color-coding fire hydrants is to help firefighters identify water requirements of fire hydrants. I have listed the national guidelines for fire hydrant colors below for a matter of interest.

Barrel	Water Supply
White	Public water supply
Yellow	Privately owned water from a public water supply
Red	Water for special use only
Violet	Water is supplied from a pond or lake

Outlet plugs	Pressures	Notes
Green	>120 psi	Extremely high pressure
Orange	50 to 120 psi	Normal pressure
Red	<50 psi	Low pressure and must be connect to the fire engine

Bonnet	Water Flow	Notes
Black	<299 GPM	-
Red	300 to 500 GPM	Inadequate water flow or out of service
Orange	500 to 1000 GPM	Marginal water flow
Green	1,000 to 1,500 GPM	Water for residential use
Blue	>1,500 GPM	Good water flow

Markings on the pavement indicate the direction of water flow to a hydrant.

Marking	Notes
Orange arrow	Water flow direction from dead-end water main
Orange arrow and vertical bar	Last hydrant plus flow direction from dead-end main
Orange 'R' in circle	Hydrant on a regulated zone
Red roman numerals	Location of street shut off valve

However, firefighters generally connect to hydrants that are most convenient. It appears that local communities color their fire hydrants not only for reasons of maintenance and upkeep but also in colors for aesthetics. For example, my neighboring communities color their fire hydrants as follows:

Town	Body	Side Cap	Top Cap
Falmouth	White	White	Blue
Forestdale	Red	Red	Red
Bourne	Orange	White	White
Buzzards Bay	Red	Red	White
Centerville	Green	White	White
Cotuit	Green	Green	White
Hyannis	Red	Green	White
Mashpee	Blue	White	White
Osterville	Green	White	White

You may find that hydrant colors in your town and adjoining communities are of different colors.

Foucault (Foo-Koh) Pendulum

Everyone loves a Foucault pendulum. The Foucault pendulum was invented by French physicist Jean Bernard Léon Foucault in 1851 and displays the earth's rotation. Flat-earth enthusiast need to take note. To start a Foucault pendulum swinging, the heavy bob at the bottom of the string is first held at an angle by a string. The string is then burned to slowly release the bob. Any other method to swing the bob, such as cutting the string or holding the bob at an angle by hand then releasing it, could result in an undesirable movement of the bob. The length of the string used in a Foucault pendulum is critical. The longer the string, the longer the swing and the more effective the Foucault pendulum behaves. For example, a one-inch string would not display any rotation of Earth.

Suppose you were physically at the top of a one-hundred-foot-long string attached to the top of a structure that is permanently fastened to Earth. There would be a heavy iron bob attached to the bottom of the string. The bob would appear stationary but moving relative to Earth's rotation because you and the string are essentially attached to Earth by means of the structure. However, if you cause the bob to swing back and forth, the frequency of the bob would then overcome the relatively lower frequency of Earth's rotation while the bob is being forced to the center of Earth by Earth's gravity. With sand spread level on the floor or ground under the bob and with a point protruding from the bottom of the bob, the point is used to etch a pattern into the sand, thus representing and displaying Earth's rotation.

With a Foucault pendulum setup on the North Pole, the pattern drawn in the sand would be circular. A Foucault pendulum setup on the equator would reveal no pattern. However, with a Foucault pendulum set up at forty-five degrees latitude, there would be a wide "daisy flower" petal pattern in the sand. Similarly, a Foucault pendulum setup on latitudes between forty-five degrees and ninety degrees would display progressively weaker daisy patterns in the sand and similarly between forty-five degrees and the equator.

Heat Pumps

Heat pumps transfer heat from one place to another. They work on the principle that heat always exists in air even at extremely low temperatures. In the winter, a heat pump extracts heat from outside air and delivers it inside. In the summer, it works in reverse, extracting heat from inside and deliver it outside. Heat pumps give off less heat at one time than a conventional gas or oil-fired furnace. This means:

- they provide even distribution of heat,
- stay on longer, and
- circulate more air throughout the home.

They're controlled by the same type of thermostat used with forced air and other heating systems. However, on very cold days, a heat pump must work especially hard to collect heat.

Mini split heat pumps

A mini split heat pump is a ductless heating, ventilating, and air-cooling system (HVACS) that does not use or require your home or building to have ductwork. Mini split heat pumps are generally used to warm or cool only one room. However, several models allow inside units to be installed in up to four rooms using four zones, all of which run from a common outside heat pump.

A mini split heat pump systems works by using an inside air handling unit and an outside outdoor compressor/condenser unit. The outside compressor heats or cools the outside air then sends the air directly to the inside air handling unit. The inside and outside units are connected together via a refrigerant line as opposed to connecting via typical ductwork.

Here are the advantages of a ductless mini split:

- Compact size
- Easy installation
- Multiple units with individual thermostat controls
- Remote control
- Serves as air conditioning *and* heating
- Saves money and energy
- No ductwork
- Tax credits and rebates
- High efficiency
- Advanced technologies

International Date Line

The International Date Line was decided at the International Meridian Conference in 1884 in Washington, DC, and is an imaginary line of longitude from the north pole to the south pole directly opposite the zero-degree longitudinal prime meridian in Greenwich, England. Longitudinal lines west of Greenwich run from 0 to 180 degrees. Longitudinal lines east of Greenwich also run from 0 to 180 degrees. Both 180 degree longitude lines form the International Date Line where the western and eastern hemispheres meet.

The IDL runs through the Pacific Ocean and is the first place on Earth where the date advances by one day as Earth rotates past the midnight position. All other locations on Earth reach a new day following the International Date Line. However, should you step behind the IDL, you will return to the previous day. The date line is not straight but instead, it makes right and left zigzags around landmasses. For example, Cape Dezhnev in Russia is one day ahead of Cape Prince of Wales in Alaska even though they are only fifty miles apart. The IDL is not governed by international law as different countries may choose the date and time zone they wish to observe.

Leap Year

What's a leap year? Earth takes one year or approximately 365.23 days to orbit around the sun. That's approximately six hours longer than 365 days established in our annual calendar. To make up this "lost time," an extra twenty-four hours is added to our calendar on every fourth year in the month of February called a "leap day." Why the month of February? Because during ancient times, February was selected as the month to include the extra day after many arguments and disagreements over religious and political issues.

Without a leap day, the dates of the equinoxes (spring on March 21 and fall on September 21) and the dates of the solstices (summer on June 21 and winter on December 21) would gradually shift to a later date on the calendar each year, then centuries from now, dates of the seasons would be much different. We would then ski during the summer months and have beach time during the winter months.

Liquor Contents

Did you ever wonder what "proof" or "ABV" on liquor labels mean? The percentage of the alcohol by volume (ABV) is half the percentage of the alcohol proof or the percentage of alcohol proof is double the percentage of the alcohol by volume.

Alcohol Proof	Alcohol by Volume (ABV)
200%	100% Ethanol
192%	96% Poland (strongest in the US)
150%	75% Rum/Tequila
100%	50% Whiskey, Vodka
80%	40% Whiskey, Gin
60%	30% Anisette/Gin
50%	25% Tequila
34%	17% Irish Cream
24%	12% Wine
20%	10% Port, Sherry wines
10%	5% Beer
5%	2.5% Beer

The following are the freezing points:

- 190% proof = -173°F (-114°C)
- 80% proof = -17°F (-27°C)
- 64% proof = -10°F (-23°C)

Navy Bell "on Watch" Time

A unique bell system was developed and used by the navy for sailors to schedule their watch duty, as well as for other naval ceremonies and events. A "watch" would start at the sound of eight bells and end four hours later at the sound of the next eight bells. Bell sounds were always in groups of two bells. For example, four bells would sound like "ding-ding (pause) ding-ding (pause) ding-ding (pause) ding-ding." Five bells would have an extra "ding-ding."

Time	Bells
12:00 Midnight	8 Bells
12:30 AM	1 Bell
1:00 AM	2 Bells
1:30 AM	3 Bells
2:00 AM	4 Bells
2:30 AM	5 Bells
3:00 AM	6 Bells
3:30 AM	7 Bells
4:00 AM	8 Bells
4:30 AM	1 Bell
5:00 AM	2 Bells
5:30 AM	3 Bells
6:00 AM	4 Bells
6:30 AM	5 Bells
7:00 AM	6 Bells
7:30 AM	7 Bells
8:00 AM	8 Bells
8:30 AM	1 Bell
9:00 AM	2 Bells
9:30 AM	3 Bells
10:00 AM	4 Bells
10:30 AM	5 Bells
11:00 AM	6 Bells
11:30 AM	7 Bells

Time	Bells
12:00 Noon	8 Bells
12:30 PM	1 Bell
1:00 PM	2 Bells
1:30 PM	3 Bells
2:00 PM	4 Bells
2:30 PM	5 Bells
3:00 PM	6 Bells
3:30 PM	7 Bells
4:00 PM	8 Bells
4:30 PM	1 Bell
5:00 PM	2 Bells
5:30 PM	3 Bells
6:00 PM	4 Bells
6:30 PM	5 Bells
7:00 PM	6 Bells
7:30 PM	7 Bells
8:00 PM	8 Bells
8:30 PM	1 Bell
9:00 PM	2 Bells
9:30 PM	3 Bells
10:00 PM	4 Bells
10:30 PM	5 Bells
11:00 PM	6 Bells
11:30 PM	7 Bells
12:00 Midnight	8 Bells

The pattern repeats.

Nuclear Reactor

What happens inside a nuclear power plant? Nuclear reactors are the heart of a nuclear power plant and use uranium for its fuel. The uranium is processed into pellets and stacked to form sealed fuel rods, which produce heat through a process called fission (fishin') where atoms split and release energy. The heat created by fission converts water to steam to run a turbine, which generates carbon-free electricity. The power level of a nuclear reactor is determined by the quantity of fuel rods used. Typically, a reactor will use over two hundred uranium rods.

If you could follow the electrical current flow from the television plugged into your wall outlet, the current from one slot in the wall outlet will flow through a transformer on a utility pole then through miles of power line wiring to a generator inside a nuclear power plant. Then from the generator along the return trip back through the utility transformer and to the slot of the same wall outlet to your television to complete the circuit (cycle). Although this cycle may cover an incredible distance, the distance covered by electrons flowing while running your television during your lifetime amounts to less than an inch.

Old Glory

When my family migrated from Italy to the United States, one of the first things they did was study to become US citizens. I studied along with them. One of the lessons I learned that remained with me to this day was the colors of our flag. Since then, I've had discussions with friends about the colors of "old glory" only to learn that very few knew what the colors actually stand for. Here's a reminder.

The stripes stand for the original thirteen colonies. The stars represent our fifty states. Among many, red symbolizes courage, readiness, and the bloodshed by those who fought to protect and to defend our freedom and democracy. White represents purity, unity, and hold to our ideals. Blue (navy blue) signifies vigilance and justice for all.

Police Radar Guns

How do they Work?

Radar (RAdio Detection And Ranging) is electronic equipment that is designed to transmit radio frequencies (RF) transmissions directed to then reflected off objects to return information about the object, such as speed, direction, shape, size, location, distance covered, and even the composition of the object. Early radar speed guns around 1947 used vacuum tube equipment which were large, heavy, and cumbersome. These old radar guns transmitted on frequencies around 2.455 gigahertz (GHz) referred to as the S-band.

Radar guns used in the 1960s transmitted on frequencies around 10.525 GHz (X-band), and around 1976, radar guns began transmitting on frequencies of 24.125 and 24.150 GHz (K-band). The problems experienced with K-band was it was close to a band of frequencies absorbed by water and as a result was strongly diminished by atmospheric moisture in fog and heavy rain.

Today, traffic radar guns almost always use the K-band on any one of thirteen channels from 33.4 GHz to 36.0 GHz in either narrow or wideband mode. Higher frequencies are preferred as they have a narrower beam width, which improves range and accuracy.

There are three main traffic radar modes. (1) Continuous-wave (CW) radars are always turned on and are used for unattended operation, such as in roadside displays with LED speed displays that display vehicle speed. (2) Pulsed mode radars, which transmit a short pulse every few seconds with the timing being set by the operator. An intermittent pulse provides a level of defense against radar detectors and are generally used for continuous traffic monitoring while police cruisers are in motion and frequently used during unattended operation. (3) Instant-on radar is manually triggered by the police officer parked at a roadside and typically a gun-type device that can be hand carried anywhere. Radar detectors are rendered virtually useless against instant-on radar guns.

Doppler effect

The doppler effect used in these radar systems make use of a change in its reflected frequency caused by a moving object; for example, the rise in the pitch of a train horn as it approaches then the fall of pitch once the train horn passes. This rising and falling pitch associated with motion is referred to as the doppler effect. Here is what happens:

Understanding that the speed of sound is approximately 760 MPH (depending on temperature, air pressure, wind, and humidity) and with a train horn frequency of, say, 1 kilohertz (KHz) and the speed of the train, say, 22 MPH, let's visit what happens while the train moves toward us. The clock starts when the peak of the first horn sound reaches our ears. The next peak is due seconds later, but since the train is moving toward us, the next peak arrives slightly sooner. And with the wavelength being shorter, the horn pitch rises.

Doppler radar guns use this same principle to measure vehicle speed, using microwaves in lieu of sound. The radar is aimed at the traffic, and the control unit measures the difference between the frequency of the transmitted signal against the frequency of the reflected signal. It considers the speed of the police car and displays the result as the speed of the car being targeted.

It doesn't matter if the targeted vehicle is moving toward or away from the radar as the doppler effect is only concerned with the difference in frequency between the transmitted and reflected signals and the speed of the police car to perform its calculations. Unfortunately, errors of the doppler effect may be caused by its radar signal striking the targeted vehicle at an angle. Some doppler systems can compensate for this type of error by manually inputting the degree of the angle.

Police officers are specially trained and certified to operate these units and must be periodically recertified. Part of the training includes learning how to ensure that the vehicle the officer thinks is being targeted is actually the one the radar is measuring. The radar units themselves can help in this regard by displaying information, such as the speed of the strongest return target and the speed of the fastest target. The strongest return is usually from the nearest vehicle, all else being equal.

Larger vehicles, such as tractor trailers, will return a stronger signal as well, but these can also be readily identified visually. Visual cues are important in other ways, such as noticing that one vehicle is obviously traveling faster than the others on the road. Using visual information, displayed readings and other techniques, the officer can establish with high confidence that the intended target is the one actually being measured.

Radar units must be periodically calibrated and recertified. Certifications for both the unit and the operator may need to be presented in court if a motorist contests a speeding violation. In short, a number of safeguards and checks are in place to ensure that radars are used properly and effectively and that the information acquired is accurate and interpreted correctly.

Power Line Buzz

Why do power lines buzz?

The buzzing sound that you occasionally hear comes from overhead high voltage power lines is caused whenever a discharge of energy from the electrical field around conductor surfaces becomes greater than the breakdown strength of the air surrounding the conductor. This discharge results in a visible glow of light near the conductor known as corona discharge. The intensity of the corona discharge is determined by the atmospheric humidity, air density, wind, rain, drizzle, and fog.

Water increases the conductivity of the air, the intensity of the discharge, and the level of the sound. The intensity of the corona discharge is also determined by irregularities of the conductor surfaces, such as cracks in the insulation, nicks, or sharp points on the connectors.

However, aging or weathering of the conductors tend to reduce these factors and thus reduce or eliminate the sound. Although high voltages transmission lines have been modified so that during dry conditions they operate below the corona voltages and minimize corona-related noise. In foul weather conditions, however, corona discharges can still be caused by water droplets, fog, and snow.

Rainbows

Tell me the best way to see a rainbow!

The sun must always be on your back side. Look forward and view an imaginary line from your eyes to the shadow of your head on the ground in front of you. Now look up forty degrees from your head shadow to see the lower blue band of the rainbow (the ultraviolet end of the color spectrum) and up forty-two degrees to see the upper red band of the rainbow (the infrared end of the color spectrum). You will not see any rainbow colors at angles above forty-two degrees or below forty degrees.

Snowmaker

Have you ever wondered how ski resorts make snow for their trails? Snow making machines are placed or installed next to ski trails. Air enters the machines while water is pumped into the machines. The machines atomize the water into tiny water droplets, which are then blown into the air. The natural outside conditions will freeze the droplets if the air temperature is thirty degrees or below. If the temperature is only slightly below the freezing temperature, additional cooling units may be necessary to help speed the freezing process.

Many ski resorts install high tower structures that elevate the snow guns well above the slopes to allow the water droplets sufficient time to freeze before falling on the ski trails. Elevated snow guns are not only less disruptive to skiers, but they provide snow falling from overhead to simulate a natural environment. Some ski resorts also accumulate piles of their man-made snow for their snow trails then use snow grooming equipment to enhance the snow making process.

Sun Protection Factor (SPF)

The SPF (sun protection factor) is a multiplication factor on sunscreen products that indicates how long one can be exposed to the sun before absorbing UVB radiations, which is involved with tanning and sunburn of the skin. If you typically burn after fifteen minutes in the sun, then using a sunscreen with an SPF of 10 would delay or resist the burning process for ten times longer or for 150 minutes. However, typical SPF sunscreens do not protect against UVA, which penetrates deeper into the skin and can cause cancer as well as premature aging of the skin.

Broad spectrum protection

If the SPF label stipulates "broad spectrum protection," the sunscreen will protect against both UVB and UVA radiation. Look for PARSOL 1789 ingredient on the sunscreen label.

Sunblock

Sunblock reflects or scatters sunlight away from your skin altogether and essentially blocks the sun. The reflective particles in sunblock usually consist of zinc oxide or titanium oxide as the main ingredient. The particles in sunblock reflect both UVA and UVB radiation.

Sundial

A sundial in the garden looks great, and at the same time enhances any yard, patio, or garden. If your sundial is simply resting in one spot and not being used to tell time, you might consider setting it up to actually tell time. It's fun, simple, and useful. If you're like me, I never wear my watch or smartphone while working in the garden. Those devices don't agree with wet soil and water, not to mention sweat. For time, I rely on my sundial. To set up your sundial, use a compass and simply rotate the sundial until the shadow bar and the twelve o'clock mark face north.

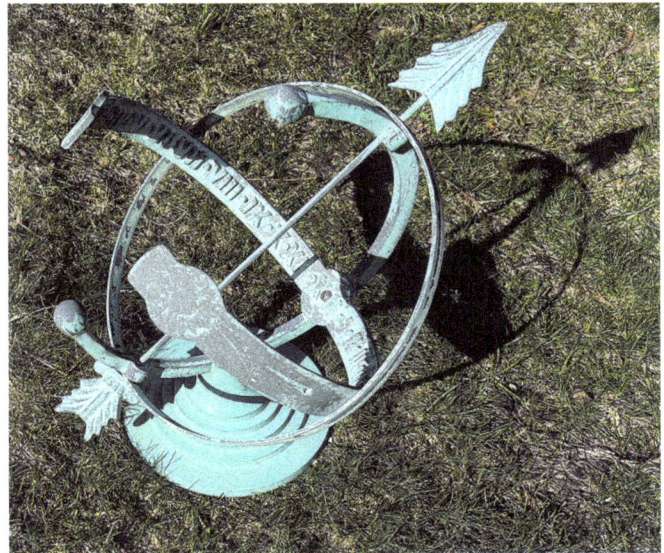

Sundial in author's yard
(Photo by the author)

Now since the sun is synchronized with true north (geographical north), use your compass and rotate the sundial an additional fifteen degrees counterclockwise. You need to do this because true north is about fifteen degrees east of magnetic north. Note that while using your compass, keep away from any ferrous metal. Your sundial will now keep accurate time. Its shadow will always cross (transit) from west to east at solar noon regardless of seasons.

Will a sundial read say 10:00 AM during all seasons even when the sun rises and sets in different locations on the horizon? Yes!

While facing the sundial, the shadow will move from left to right as the sun moves from right to left, but the shadow will not move up or down as the sun moves up or down on the horizon during the different seasons.

You can see how this works from this simple example. Tape a sheet of white paper to a wall. Place dots horizontally on the paper and mark the dots for each hour: 6:00 AM on far left, continuing to 12:00 noon in the center, and 6:00 PM on far right. Fasten a pencil vertically on a table in front of the wall. From about three feet away from the pencil. Wide beam is better than a narrow beam. Shine a flashlight (representing the sun) directly on the pencil to cast its shadow on the wall. Now keeping the flashlight on the pencil, move the flashlight right to left, and the shadow will move across the hourly dots from left to right. Now, move the flashlight up and down while on any dot, and you'll see that the shadow will remain fixed on that dot. During the various seasons, the sun rises and sets in different locations on the horizon and will not affect the time readings on sundials. For example, if you cast the shadow on the 10:00 AM dot and move the flashlight up and down, the shadow will remain on 10:00 AM. So what have we learned from this experiment? We learned that the sun's shadow on the sundial will read the time regardless of seasons.

Touchscreens

How do computer, smartphone, and iPad touchscreens work by a simple touch? The surface of a touchscreen is covered with a matrix of electrodes, such that wherever our finger(s) touch the screen, a capacitive action from our fingers influences the circuitry at the touched matrix location to complete various circuits, thus causing the associated function to execute.

Transcendental Meditation (TM)

Have you ever practiced transcendental meditation? TM was introduced in 1958 from ancient India by Maharishi Mahesh Yogi and involves the repetition of specific sounds called mantras. The technique enables the practitioner's mind to transcend to a state of restful alertness without the concentration or interference of other thoughts. Transcendental Meditation technique has spread through-out the world to become a world-wide movement.

Procedures and theory

The Transcendental Meditation technique is practiced for twenty minutes twice a day while one sits with their eyes closed. A distinguishing feature of this meditation practice is its lack of effort. The learning process requires a fee of several thousand dollars. Transcendental Meditation makes use of the natural response of the mind. When the mind settles down during the Transcendental Meditation technique, a state of restful alertness is experienced. This perception leads to a devotion and love for creation, nature, and its creator.

While attending college classes at night, I found that by practicing TM every night, I could "recharge my batteries," and I was able to continue with my studies night after night before retiring. Although I have practiced Transcendental Meditation for many years, I do not practice the conventional method as described above. Instead, I developed my own simplified technique, which works well for me and "fits" my needs. Using my version, I always accomplish my goals.

Whenever I have work to do, or work to finish, but I'm too tired to continue, I start my Transcendental Meditation, and when completed, I am at the relaxed state necessary to continue with my work or with my studies. I practice Transcendental Meditation whenever I feel the need and not on a regular schedule. As soon as I have a need for Transcendental Meditation, I enter my music room (always use a room in which you are most comfortable). I sit in my chair for twenty minutes with cell phone turned off. I keep my eyes open and the room light on to lessen the temptation to fall asleep. I relax my eyes by not focusing on objects.

The room remains perfectly silent. I slowly and nonverbally repeat my "secret" word over and over to encourage positive and peaceful thoughts. As peaceful thoughts begin to settle in, my mind becomes restful. I keep a silent clock in the room to make sure I remain in this state until "time is up." Try it. It works, but you need to be patient. At first, many thoughts will disrupt your progress, and that's all right; it's even expected. However, patience will "pay off."

Train Wheels

Have you ever wondered how trains turn around curves without the use of a steering wheel? Train wheels are typically connected together by a fixed axle. This means that the wheels on the right and left sides of the axle always turn together and at the same speed. However, during a curve, one of the wheels must cover more distance than its opposite wheel. So how do locomotives stay on the rails while rounding a curve? Where the wheels meet the track, train wheels are beveled to make their diameters bigger on the inside of the rail and smaller on the outside. This means that when the train turns left or right on a curve, the wheels that have to travel a greater distance have the greater diameter. The inner flange on wheels prevents the train from going too far and derailing. The end result is a train that stays on the tracks during turns.

About the Author

A native of Newton, Massachusetts, Ben was born in 1933 and was raised to respect his elders, respect authority, and to follow rules—a great start in learning what life is about. Ya know, "take the bad with the good!" Ben enjoyed working hard, being very active, and getting involved in areas of music, astronomy, physics, ham radio, exercise, sports, among many other interests and activities. He found that all these activities allowed him to see purpose and benefits that caused his mind to create many positive thoughts, which formed a path to his exciting careers and life.

Educated in electrical engineering, Ben worked for many major industrial firms, including the Redstone and Jupiter-C missiles with Dr. von Braun's division at Chrysler Missile, Sparrow and Hawk missiles at Raytheon Laboratories, Missile Master Air Defense System using underground Nike missiles at Martin Marietta, and research and development at Burroughs Corporation on the world's first computers. Ben's careers finally took him to Dr. Armand Hammer's Occidental Petroleum for developing large DC power systems. Among Ben's major accomplishments were his design and development of an electrical power distribution center (PDC); development of the first printed circuit boards at Raytheon Labs; six company level patents, two personal US patents pending; and three published books. His first book, *Nobska*, was published in May 2021. His second book, *Nobska 2nd Edition*, was published in June 2023, and this third novel, *Thoughts*, was published in 2024. Ben is currently writing his fourth book.

A US Air Force Korean veteran, Ben was a crew chief on an F-86D Sabre jet fighter electronic flight simulator and proud to have been assigned and served in the same squadron of the famed WWI ace, Eddie Rickenbacker's "Hat in the Ring" 94th Fighter Interceptor Squadron. Ben raised three wonderful children and is now retired on Cape Cod, Massachusetts, with his lovely and talented wife, Joanne Blum-Carnevale.

Printed in the USA
CPSIA information can be obtained
at www.ICGtesting.com
LVHW070306291024
794844LV00004B/6/J